KT-456-595

Overcoming Common Problems

Coping with Eating Disorders and Body Image

Christine Craggs-Hinton

sheldon**PRESS**

First published in Great Britain in 2006
Sheldon Press
36 Causton Street
London SW1P 4ST

Copyright © Christine Craggs-Hinton 2006

All rights reserved. No part of this book may be reproduced
or transmitted in any form or by any means,
electronic or mechanical, including photocopying,
recording, or by any information storage and retrieval system,
without permission in writing from the publisher.

British Library Cataloguing-in-Publication Data

A catalogue record for this book is available from the British Library

ISBN-13: 978–0–85969–966–2
ISBN-10: 0–85969–966–8

1 3 5 7 9 10 8 6 4 2

Typeset by Deltatype Limited, Birkenhead, Merseyside
Printed in Great Britain by
Ashford Colour Press

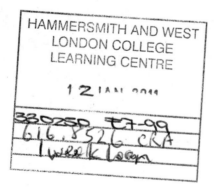

HAMMERSMITH AND WEST
LONDON COLLEGE
LEARNING CENTRE

1 2 JAN 2011

330250   £7-99
616.8526 CRA
1 week loan

CHRISTINE CRAGGS-HINTON, mother of three, followed a career in the Civil Service until, in 1991, she developed fibromyalgia, a chronic pain condition. Christine took up writing for therapeutic reasons and has, in the past few years, produced *Living with Fibromyalgia*, *The Fibromyalgia Healing Diet*, *The Chronic Fatigue Healing Diet*, *Coping with Polycystic Ovary Syndrome*, *Coping with Gout* and *How to Beat Pain* (all published by Sheldon Press). She also writes for the Fibromyalgia Association UK and the related *FaMily* magazine. In recent years she has also become interested in fiction writing.

THE LEARNING CENTRE
HAMMERSMITH AND WEST
LONDON COLLEGE
GLIDDON ROAD
LONDON W14 9BL

WITHDRAWN

HAMMERSMITH WEST LONDON COLLEGE

330250

Overcoming Common Problems Series

Selected titles
A full list of titles is available from Sheldon Press,
36 Causton Street, London SW1P 4ST, and on our website at
www.sheldonpress.co.uk

Overcoming Common Problems Series

Overcoming Common Problems Series

Living with Crohn's Disease
Dr Joan Gomez

Living with Diabetes
Dr Joan Gomez

Living with Fibromyalgia
Christine Craggs-Hinton

Living with Food Intolerance
Alex Gazzola

Living with Grief
Dr Tony Lake

Living with Heart Disease
Victor Marks, Dr Monica Lewis and
Dr Gerald Lewis

Living with High Blood Pressure
Dr Tom Smith

Living with Hughes Syndrome
Triona Holden

Living with Loss and Grief
Julia Tugendhat

Living with Lupus
Philippa Pigache

Living with Nut Allergies
Karen Evennett

Living with Osteoarthritis
Dr Patricia Gilbert

Living with Osteoporosis
Dr Joan Gomez

Living with Rheumatoid Arthritis
Philippa Pigache

Living with Sjögren's Syndrome
Sue Dyson

Losing a Baby
Sarah Ewing

Losing a Child
Linda Hurcombe

Make Up or Break Up: Making the Most of Your Marriage
Mary Williams

Making Friends with Your Stepchildren
Rosemary Wells

Making Relationships Work
Alison Waines

Overcoming Anger
Dr Windy Dryden

Overcoming Anxiety
Dr Windy Dryden

Overcoming Back Pain
Dr Tom Smith

Overcoming Depression
Dr Windy Dryden and Sarah Opie

Overcoming Impotence
Mary Williams

Overcoming Jealousy
Dr Windy Dryden

Overcoming Loneliness and Making Friends
Márianna Csóti

Overcoming Procrastination
Dr Windy Dryden

Overcoming Shame
Dr Windy Dryden

The PMS Diet Book
Karen Evennett

Rheumatoid Arthritis
Mary-Claire Mason and Dr Elaine Smith

The Self-Esteem Journal
Alison Waines

Shift Your Thinking, Change Your Life
Mo Shapiro

Stress at Work
Mary Hartley

Ten Steps to Positive Living
Dr Windy Dryden

Think Your Way to Happiness
Dr Windy Dryden and Jack Gordon

The Traveller's Good Health Guide
Ted Lankester

Understanding Obsessions and Compulsions
Dr Frank Tallis

When Someone You Love Has Depression
Barbara Baker

Your Man's Health
Fiona Marshall

Contents

Introduction

A poor body image is so widespread in our society that it's almost considered normal. Studies have shown that body image problems can begin in childhood, children as young as seven and eight years old being concerned about their weight and appearance. How has this happened? The massive media coverage of the 'perfect' body and the 'perfect' face must take at least some of the responsibility.

There are few people on TV, in films, in advertising and in glossy magazines who are not ideal physical specimens - 'ideal' being very slender with C or D cup breasts and glamorous good looks for a woman, and of athletic build with nice looks and good muscle definition for a man. It is teenagers, however, who are most vulnerable to images of 'perfection' in the media. At a time when hormones are raging and their bodies changing, their looks and build are ultra-important to them and unfortunately they tend to judge themselves on these things rather than on their achievements or their values and beliefs. It's a sad fact that most would give anything to be slim and good-looking. Indeed, some would choose a good physical appearance over passing any number of exams and being able to go on to a successful career.

When a poor body image is combined with low self-esteem – due to a difficult family life or early trauma perhaps – children and teenagers can start to distort their bodies or faces in their minds. A girl might be the right weight for her height, but the person she sees in the mirror is distinctly overweight and full of lumps and bumps. She may start a catastrophic diet, virtually starving herself, so the weight drops off her and she looks quite skeletal. It's difficult for her to begin eating properly again, as well, as she feels certain it will make her 'huge'. Individuals with bulimia are desperate to be and stay slim and try hard to diet. However, emotional pain, stress, anxiety or just plain boredom can trigger them to binge-eat huge amounts of food. They then make themselves sick or use laxatives so they don't put on weight. Compulsive eaters try diet after diet in an attempt to lose weight, then, when the effort gets too much or they feel stressed and anxious, they will find themselves bingeing. They only differ from bulimics in that they don't make themselves sick or use other forms of purging.

Body Dysmorphic Disorder is another manifestation of low self-esteem and internalized emotional pain; and like anorexia, it is another condition of mental distortion. In this instance, the person imagines defects in his or her face, hair and parts of the body. A young man of normal appearance might spend hours grooming himself in the morning, wanting the image in the mirror to be perfect and never being satisfied. During his working day, he feels anxiously compelled to keep checking the mirror to see whether his tiny bald patch is showing, whether his nose looks any bigger than it did, whether his skin is still 'too blotchy'. Seeing a male model on a placard at lunchtime may intensify his anxiety and even bring on a panic attack. There are many others with Body Dysmorphic Disorder who feel so hideous they can't bear for others to see them and stay hidden indoors.

Because an addiction to alcohol is often caused by low self-esteem and emotional pain, it is discussed in this book, too. Alcohol abuse is a huge problem in today's world, with one in four adults frequently drinking quantities that can be dangerous to their health. Alcohol is a relaxant; it releases inhibitions and can ensure a good time in the company of others. However, when alcohol is used to blot out emotional pain, it is easy to become addicted and that's no fun at all.

Fortunately, there are excellent medical and psychological treatments for each of these disorders, all of which are discussed in this book.

1

Body Image in the Twenty-First Century

Studies suggest that 80 per cent of women are dissatisfied with their bodies. This is a staggering number, for it is known that our body image is crucial to our happiness and even to our state of health. Those of us with a positive body image have a real and honest perception of our weight and shape and feel comfortable with our appearance. Those of us with a negative body image have a distorted perception of our weight and shape; we tend to compare our bodies with others and, as a result, feel awkward and anxious.

Strangely, a positive body image doesn't demand a 'perfect' body. There are many who are far from the shape we idealize today, yet who have a positive body image. Conversely, there are many others with what is perceived as a good body who possess a negative body image.

The same applies exactly to looks and hair. Individuals who feel happy about these things aren't necessarily beautiful and with long gleaming tresses, neither are those with a negative viewpoint ugly or have hair that is dull and unmanageable.

What exactly does 'body image' mean?

The image we have of our own appearance is always changing and involves our perception, imagination, emotions and physical sensations. It is not based on fact, but is psychological in nature, and is influenced much more by confidence and self-esteem than by actual physical attractiveness as judged by others.

Our body image evolves from virtually every experience we have as we are growing and developing. This includes the way our parents interacted with us, whom we chose as our role models and whether we were teased about our appearance by our peers. So what exactly does 'body image' mean? It is best described as a combination of the following:

- *How we feel about our physical appearance.* For example, a boy may feel that his ribcage is too thin and wish he owned the much-revered 'six-pack'.

3

- *How we feel about certain parts of our bodies.* For example, a girl may believe that her nose is too bumpy, her lips too thin, her legs too short, and so on.
- *How we think others see us.* For example, many people are convinced that others see them as ugly, as in Body Dysmorphic Disorder, or overweight, as in anorexia and bulimia.
- *Our perception of our physical appearance.* For example, individuals with anorexia are widely documented as having a distorted image of their bodies. They see themselves as fat when they are painfully thin. Likewise, people with Body Dysmorphic Disorder can see themselves as ugly when in fact they have a perfectly pleasant appearance.
- *Mood at a particular time.* For example, when we are feeling happy, we are more likely to be able to accept our general appearance. When we are feeling depressed, we can hate our general appearance.
- *The social climate at the time.* For example, in the present western social climate, beauty and slimness are admired in a woman, whereas men with good muscle definition are held in high regard.

Personality traits

Individuals with a negative body image are likely to have the following personality traits:

- They don't like themselves very much.
- They are hard on themselves.
- They may feel like 'losers'.
- They believe the media myth that you need to be thin to be taken seriously, to 'fit in'.

Body image and childhood

It is in childhood that the perception of a person's body begins to evolve. A positive body image can gradually be established when parents are comfortable with their own bodies and confident in general. On the other hand, a negative body image can be instilled when parents – particularly the mother – are not satisfied with their appearance, and are concerned about their weight, and struggle with self-esteem.

A child's body image will also evolve based on how often he or she is held and touched. One who is deprived of touch may not develop the sensory information required to form an accurate understanding of his or her body shape and size. Surprisingly, this is capable of translating to the child's eating senses, as a result of which they can find it difficult to know when they have eaten enough, and fully satisfied their hunger. On the other extreme, a child who is sexually abused may feel shame and loathing towards his or her body. This, too, is capable of translating to the child's eating senses.

The image a child forms of his or her body will generally withstand through to adulthood.

Learning by example

Recent surveys show that children are becoming obsessed about their appearance at younger and younger ages. The National Eating Disorders Association of America recently carried out studies into dieting behaviour in youngsters and found that 42 per cent of girls aged 5 to 8 would like to be thinner, 51 per cent of 9 and 10 year old girls feel better about themselves when they are on a diet, and 46 per cent of 9 to 11 year old girls are 'sometimes' or 'very often' on diets. Of these children, 82 per cent of their families are 'sometimes' or 'very often' on diets. Sadly, these children can only have been influenced by parents and friends, and by the images of 'perfection' blasted out by the media. Children have minds like sponges. Indeed, some of the information they absorb would shock and appal their parents. However, a good deal of that information is likely to originate from the parents themselves.

When a mother talks about dieting, her child can be eager to copy her. Research has shown that daughters in particular are more likely to consider dieting when they know their mother is dieting. They can even soak up comments about dieting concepts such as limiting saturated fat and cutting out carbohydrates. However, although adults need little saturated fat and their bodies can cope with restricted carbohydrates for a while, a child needs to eat all food groups in order to grow and develop correctly – and that includes saturated fat.

In one study that looked at girls' ideas on dieting, a five-year-old declared, 'When you're on a diet, you can't eat.' That's another thing about children – they are apt to misunderstand.

The attitude of others

A child also soaks up the attitude of others regarding his or her body and looks. One who is teased about his or her looks by other children is likely to incorporate that into a negative body image, as described by psychologist L. C. Kolb. I remember that a close friend of mine at school was quite overweight and often called hurtful names by our peers. She frequently told me that she despised her body.

I recall another schoolfriend who developed breasts much earlier than the other girls and who then drew unwanted sexual attention from the older boys. The girl wore baggy jumpers in an effort to conceal her large breasts, but the lecherous remarks still flowed. By the time we other girls had begun developing, she had put on nearly two stone in weight, effectively making herself less sexually attractive, as judged at the time.

After being made a spectacle of or drawing comments that are derogatory, adolescents are as open as children to starting to dislike their appearance. This dislike is liable to carry through to adulthood. In fact, the girl who developed breasts early has remained overweight all her adult life and I wonder if that unwelcome attention so long ago is the deep-rooted cause.

When parents make derogatory comments

The attitude of parents towards their child's body and looks is also integrated into the child's body image, any criticism having an acutely negative effect. At family gatherings, my father used to point out my bony knees and say laughingly that they were just like his. Although I laughed along with him, I was soon feeling intensely ashamed of these particular body parts and would do anything I could to cover them up – I wouldn't even wear shorts on holiday. My father would have been horrified if he'd known how he made me feel, if he had known that his words had left me with a lifelong fixation. I think he was trying to say it was his fault not my own that my knees were bony, but it translated as a put-down to me.

Help your child to develop a positive body image

If you are a parent, it is always wise to remember that you are a role model for your children, and as such you should take care how you behave and what you say and do. Instead of trying to diet, you would be advised to follow a long-term healthy eating and exercise programme, of the type you would like your children to respect and copy. There is a sample healthy eating chart on page 95.

In order to help your children to develop a positive body image and to relate to food in a healthy way, follow these important steps:

- *Show your children that you love and value them.* If you are not a tactile person, force yourself to be – it will pay dividends! A warm hug from a parent is worth more to a child than any toy or treat.

- *Compliment your children* on their particular talents, accomplishments, values and efforts.
- *Examine your dreams and ambitions for your children.* Make certain you are not stressing looks and slimness as a way they might attain their goals.
- *Make sure your children know they can come to you with any problems they have.* Ask them about their day and be interested in their lives.
- *Avoid giving sons and daughters the message that girls are less important than boys.* For example, don't let boys off doing housework and shopping.
- *Watch television with your children and discuss the images you see.* Explain that the beautiful people in the media make up only a tiny proportion of the population and that the average adult is a little overweight with less than perfect looks.
- *Consider the way you see your own body and how this has been shaped by media images and prejudice against weight.* Discuss the ugliness of prejudice with your children and help them to understand that we all have a different genetic make-up that gives a diversity of body shapes and sizes.
- *Try to accept yourself as you are.* Daughters listen to the way their mothers talk about themselves and each other to learn the language of womanhood. They can only learn to love and accept their bodies if they see women who love and accept their own.
- *Make sure your children understand that weight gain is a normal part of development*, and that girls in particular put on weight at puberty.
- *Let your children make their own decisions about food.* If you are concerned about one or more of them not eating enough of a certain food group, try not to worry. Just make sure that nutritious food and snacks are always available. Children tend to sort themselves out, diet-wise, in the end.
- *Try to measure people by what they say and do, not by how they look.* Your children will follow your example.
- *Teach your children by example* that eating a variety of foods in well-balanced meals, three times a day, is good for health.
- *Learn all you can about the dangers of dieting* and discuss this with your children.

7

- *Avoid making negative statements* about food, weight, body size and shape.
- *Discuss with your children the importance of moderate exercise* for good health and vitality.
- *Take up daily exercise* for the buzz it gives and the knowledge that it is making your body stronger and more supple. Don't ever make overeating a reason for exercise.
- *Don't avoid an activity* – swimming, for example – because the clothing required draws attention to your shape and size.

Body image and adolescence

The natural weight gain and other body changes that girls undergo during puberty can make them dissatisfied with their bodies. The media plays a big part in causing further dissatisfaction, for female role models tend to be glamorously slim with shining good looks and perfect complexions. Teenage girls make constant comparisons with these images and strive in vain to achieve an impossible goal. In the meantime, they may despise their bodies and can tell you down to the minutest detail what's wrong with them.

In a 1997 survey, both teenage girls and boys reported that very slim or muscular models made them feel insecure about themselves (E. Wertheim, et al.). If you look at the most popular magazines on the newspaper racks, the images on the covers represent approximately 0.3 per cent of the population, leaving a massive 99.97 per cent with no chance of measuring up. Remember that looking good is a career for these people. Many have fitness trainers and nutrition advisers; plenty have even undergone cosmetic surgery to correct their 'faults'. Of course, there is then the airbrush to make any other unwanted bits vanish.

Preferred body forms through the ages

At any particular time in history, there has been a socially preferred body form, especially where women were concerned. The oldest representation of the human form ever found is the 'Venus of Wilendorf', a statue dating back to between 20,000 and 30,000 BC, which was obviously idolized. The statue is of an extremely rotund woman with enormous breasts and a huge stomach. Female figures from the Neolithic period show that excess weight was revered, and

8

there are prehistoric Egyptian, Babylonian and Greek sculptures that indicate a predilection for overweight women.

Obviously, at a time when there was an ever-present fear of starvation, these images are as likely to be symbols of abundance and fertility as they are realistic representations of their perfect woman at the time. However, there is no doubt that women with well-padded bodies have been idealized throughout modern history. It is only since the 1960s, with the adoration of Jean Shrimpton then Twiggy, that 'super-slender' has been the form of choice in the West.

The model of attractiveness in the twenty-first century

It is clear that body image disorders are in some part caused by the modern-day concept of attractiveness. Glossy magazines picturing good looks and toned bodies are bought in their millions each week, engendering that desire to be slim. People in the film world, popular culture and the media are generally lithe and lissome – is it any wonder the rest of us feel inadequate in comparison? And sadly, it's those individuals who are vulnerable, who were perhaps taunted about their looks or build as a child who are more defenceless in the face of these images, who believe themselves severely wanting in comparison.

However, the images in the media are quite simply a lie – if the people depicted have not surrendered to the surgeon's knife, their lumps and bumps have been digitally removed. Film stars like Tom Cruise and Sylvester Stallone are actually much shorter than they appear on-screen, but they are filmed carefully to make them seem taller. When cosmetics are advertised, soft-focus is used to make one woman appear wrinkle-free after using a certain cream, and to make another seem to have exquisitely clear skin when really she has not. Such camera-trickery goes on all the time. The motive is simply to sell the product, to make pots of money.

It is unfortunate that the majority of us are taken in by these images, for in doing so we allow our self-esteem to be dictated by an external factor. We let the 'media machine' make us unhappy about our appearance so that we want to change what we are. In agreeing with the narrow media definition of attractiveness, we lose our individuality and yearn desperately to 'measure up'. Recently, *People* magazine carried out a poll in which 93 per cent of female readers reported feeling so insecure they attempt repeatedly to lose weight. Moreover, 37 per cent said they were willing to try diets that pose a risk to their health and 34 per cent said they were thinking about going 'under the knife'.

In the western world, the average fashion model is 5 feet 11 inches tall and weighs 8 and a half stone, but the average woman is 5 feet 4 inches tall and weighs 10 stone. Fashion models are thinner and lighter than 98 per cent of the female population. In the UK, even the average shop mannequin is clad in a size 8 or 10. It's no wonder then that women are dissatisfied with their appearance.

It doesn't help that today's eternal promotion of the ideal shape and look sends the message to women in particular that they must be appealing on the outside to be valued by others. This can lead them to believe that the way they look is central to their happiness and success in life. But surely it's not fair that the media have such power, that it has the ability to generate a negative body image, lack of self-esteem and general unhappiness? But it is we, the consumer, who allow them that power. We allow them to sell us the message 'thin is in' many times a day through numerous avenues.

The female is more susceptible than the male

In an Australian study of high school students, it was found that 70 per cent of adolescent girls wished they were thinner in comparison with 34 per cent of boys. Indeed, it has been estimated that today's young woman sees more images of beautiful women in one day than her mother saw through her entire adolescence. It is no wonder, then, that many modern young women yearn to be like their ideal images, that they tend to think there are more beautiful people in society than there actually are.

Of course, males are also affected by media images, but not to the same degree – perhaps as there is far more variance in the male 'ideal' form. Rugby players are big and very muscular, football players can be a little shorter and less bulky and marathon runners are slim and lean – all of which are socially acceptable builds for a man. In the study quoted above, only 7 per cent of girls reported wanting to be larger, compared with 35 per cent of boys. By 'larger', I assume the boys wished to be both taller and of a greater weight – and as boys are genetically programmed to be larger than girls, this result is no surprise.

The media machine is most definitely involved in the rise of eating disorders, and far more females than males fall victim.

However, in Body Dysmorphic Disorder (BDD), it appears there are only slightly more female than male sufferers, which suggests there is more going on. (See the causes of anorexia, bulimia, compulsive overeating and BDD, in later chapters.)

When adolescents fall short of today's acceptable image

Adolescents who feel their bodies and looks fail to match up to the socially acceptable image can feel desperate. After all, this is a vulnerable time in their lives, when attractiveness is being constantly measured. They may be of pleasant appearance and of a normal weight for their height and build, but because they aren't as pretty and slim as the 'in-crowd' of girls, or as handsome and toned as the 'in-crowd' of boys, they can feel ugly and grossly overweight.

Adolescents with a negative body image are likely to fixate about a particular part of their face or body, if not their appearance as a whole. When this happens, that particular part can become larger, ugly, or their entire body can be bigger in their minds. They may also be convinced that others are constantly judging their appearance and finding them lacking.

Things you can do to improve your body image

To improve your body image, take note of the following:

- Don't ever forget that the main objective of the fashion, cosmetics, diet, fitness and cosmetic surgery industries is to make money. The ultra-thin ideal is reaping great rewards for them, but is it working for you?
- Do you look in the mirror one day and think you look good, and the next day think you look awful? It isn't your body that's changing, it's your perception of it that is. Try to notice your mood when you look in the mirror – it's odds on that you are feeling happy and content on the days you think you look good, and down in the dumps on the days you think you look awful. Women who are confident and happy know their bodies and faces don't fit the 'perfect' mould, but don't really care.
- Try to avoid discussing your particular weight problems. Every conversation of this type fixes your dissatisfaction in your head a little more. It also encourages others to be unhappy with their own bodies.
- Think of five women you most admire. How often is the woman's appearance a reason you admire her? Are your choices perhaps

swayed by our culture? What would you prefer a young woman to most admire in you – that is, in the you as you are now?

- The emphasis on slenderness is relatively new. Think of how you would feel if a well-padded form was suddenly in vogue and everyone was madly putting on weight? Would you feel they were being manipulated? But we are allowing ourselves to be manipulated now. Do you really think that struggling to attain the fashionable look and shape is worth all the heartache? Do those who fail to achieve the fashionable look and shape really deserve to feel worthless and depressed?

- Many women of today work and so have money to spend. The fashion, cosmetics and related industries want to take that money off us, and try to curry favour with us to that end. Think of how much you spend on fashion and cosmetics and ask yourself whether it reflects the person you are or the person society wants you to be. What would you spend your money on if looks weren't that important?

- Reflect on how you would prefer to spend your energy – pursuing the 'perfect body image' or enjoying family, friends, school, your job, and most importantly . . . life.

- Ask yourself if it's important that you define yourself by what popular culture dictates. Wouldn't it be fun to develop your own style – particularly if you're female? Wear gypsy skirts all the time if you want – don't if you don't want. Wear checked caps all the time if you want, don't if you don't want . . . By accepting yourself as you wish yourself to be, you are helping to loosen the grip exerted by the media machine.

- Take plenty of exercise and make sure to eat healthily. Take walks, go swimming, play tennis, join an exercise class – an activity you find enjoyable. Then go home and cook yourself a wholesome meal. If you are not a good cook, borrow a couple of recipe books from the library. Exercise and a good diet will help you to achieve the weight that is genetically correct for your body frame. They will also give you more energy, make you feel stronger and reduce any stress. (See a sample diet on page 95.)

Weight prejudice

The flip-side of worshipping slimness is having prejudice against 'weight'. Unfortunately, in our western culture, while a person who is slim is stereotyped as being active, intelligent, social and successful, a person who is overweight is stereotyped as being lazy, greedy, lacking willpower, anti-social and a failure. Many of us hold these fixed and unfair opinions and tend to judge others on them. It is largely as a result of these opinions that millions of people strive for thinness at any cost. Indeed, one eating disorders association carried out a recent survey in which 50 per cent of women stated they would prefer to be run over by a lorry than be overweight and have people despise them!

Weight prejudice can be found everywhere, from the job a person was overlooked for to the love interest who just didn't see them. If we start by dropping our own prejudices and encourage our children and the people around us to drop theirs, we are helping to make a better world.

Self-esteem

Many of us care more about our appearance than we do about our achievements, about our growth as thinking people, and success in our careers. However, few of us care about our appearance in a positive way. We either hate certain aspects of our bodies and looks, or we hate the way we look altogether. This, unfortunately, has a knock-on effect on our confidence and self-worth. People with a negative body image tend to lose sight of their positive qualities, and may misinterpret how they are coming across to others. Furthermore, they are quite likely to misread the way they are being spoken to and treated.

When your self-esteem is low due to a negative body image, it can be easy to allow an eating disorder to enter your life.

Test your self-esteem

Below is a list of statements in pairs. Go down the list, truthfully selecting the statement that suits you best:

a. Do you gladly accept compliments?
b. Do you effectively reject compliments?

a. Are there a lot of things about your appearance you like?
b. Do you look for and point out your physical shortcomings?

a. Do you respect who you are and what you have achieved?
b. Do you focus on your mistakes or bad things that have happened?

a. When you reach a goal do you feel proud of yourself?
b. When you reach a goal do you think you could have done better?

a. Do you like your friends and enjoy spending time with them?
b. Do you tolerate your friends and sometimes avoid them?

a. Do you prefer to be in company?
b. Do you prefer to be alone?

If you selected all the 'a' answers, you are likely to have high self-esteem. If you selected all the 'b' answers you are likely to have low self-esteem and need to work on feeling better about yourself. If you don't already have an eating disorder or Body Dysmorphic Disorder, you are at risk of developing one of these conditions. To help yourself, you could borrow books on self-esteem and anxiety from the library; you could attend an assertiveness class; purchase tapes on assertiveness training and relaxation techniques, and you can continue reading this book. You will hopefully learn to develop a true sense of self, rather than one that is pressed on you by outside influences. You will also learn that self-esteem doesn't depend on your appearance, but on who and what you are as a person.

If you had a mixture of 'a' answers and 'b' answers, you are not in immediate danger of developing an eating disorder or Body Dysmorphic Disorder. However, you will like yourself more as a person and get more from your life if you, too, work on your self-esteem as described above.

Distorted body image, distorted self-image

Those who imagine they are fatter or far less attractive than their counterparts are likely to have a false impression of how they are perceived.

Alice and Jodie are best friends at school. Alice is always top in exams but doesn't like being referred to as 'brainy'. She has always wanted to be one of the 'popular' girls, but feels her size and looks are preventing it. She would give anything to be slim and pretty like they are and doesn't wonder they don't have much time for her. Jodie – who is friendly with everyone – wishes Alice would accept praise for her good marks instead of being convinced that her classmates are winding her up. She says Alice has a defeatist attitude where the other girls are concerned – when she does force herself to speak to them she wrongly thinks their replies are sarcastic.

Alice has a distorted impression of the way she looks and the way others see her. She undervalues herself so much that she thinks she will only be accepted by the popular girls if she loses weight and improves her appearance. She doesn't realize that these girls look up to her for her intelligence, that they are trying to be friendly and would like to give her a chance of entering their crowd. It often happens that the slim, pretty girls are viewed as looking down on the others. In fact, they are generally as normal as any other girl and happy to make new friends.

Sliding into an eating disorder, BDD or alcoholism

Habits

We all have habits – behaviours we carry out over and over again in the same way and often in similar circumstances. For instance, the first thing I do when I get up in the morning is switch on the radio; my mother says 'touch wood' and taps her head when we expect something nice to happen; and my husband crosses his fingers when we're watching the lottery balls appear.

Whether we are aware of our habits or not, they can give structure and order to our lives and help us to feel calm and protected in different situations. Habits help us to get through the day. If you take a look at your own habits, you will see that you do things in the same order as you did the day before and the day before that. Even the way you climb into bed is likely to be habitual.

Sometimes habits can be harmful, though. A boy who is praised for eating everything on his plate will habitually clear his plate as an adult as well, even when he's not hungry – the memory of the praise feels better than the discomfort of a bloated stomach. He may then pass on this unhealthy habit to his children.

Losing control

It is when habits cause behaviours over which you lose voluntary control that you really have a problem. An occasional activity can turn into an activity that dominates your thoughts. In anorexia, bulimia and compulsive eating, an occasional diet becomes frequent dieting behaviour until at some point it takes over your life. The same thing happens with people who drink a lot of alcohol, smoke a lot of cigarettes and use a lot of drugs – the habit quickly becomes an addiction. Addictive behaviour, obsessions and compulsions are a large part of anorexia, alcoholism and Body Dysmorphic Disorder (BDD).

Your answers to the following will tell you whether your habits have become harmful addictions:

1. Is your habit so important in your life that you can't or won't function without its help?
2. Is it impossible for you to go for long without feeling an intense inner pressure to indulge in the habit?
3. Do you seem to be thinking about your habit for much of the time?

If you answered 'yes' to all three questions, your habit is no longer a simple habit. It has become one of the following:

- *An obsession.* This is defined as a thought that fills the mind continually, obtrusively and to a troubling extent.
- *A compulsion.* This is defined as feeling an internal pressure to do something repeatedly without understanding why.
- *An addiction.* This is defined as a craving or longing, due to a physical and emotional dependency on a particular thing.

If a certain behaviour can be characterized as obsessive, compulsive or addictive it is liable to disrupt your normal lifestyle, damage your physical and mental health and make life very difficult for your family and friends. It can be almost impossible to regain control without professional counselling or medical intervention.

A person with obsessive, compulsive or addictive behaviour is likely to give the object of their focus more attention than they give their families, friends, school, work or any responsibilities. Hobbies take a narrower focus until the person ends up focused only on his or her obsession. In the end, their activities are all geared to satisfying only that one thing, and their actions appear compulsive, illogical, bizarre and very resistant to change.

When obsessions, compulsions or addictions are related to food and eating, an eating disorder is likely to arise. It is at the point when food is used to express or control distress that an eating disorder is born. Food is used in an emotional context in anorexia, bulimia and compulsive eating.

2

Anorexia

Anorexia – full name, anorexia nervosa – is a psychological disorder that is ten times more common in females than in males. For simplicity, I have therefore referred to the person affected as female. The word 'anorexia' literally means 'loss of appetite' – misleading as anorexics are almost always hungry. Through sheer willpower and stubborn single-mindedness an anorexic will deny her hunger – either learning to suppress it or revelling in its discomfort as proof of her inner strength and self-control.

An intense fear of being overweight is accompanied by a distorted body image where the individual perceives herself as heavy and full of lumps and bumps. Despite everyone around her protesting that she is actually underweight – maybe even grossly underweight – she refuses to believe it and continues to diet.

People with anorexia avoid maintaining a normal body weight by severely restricting what they eat. Their regime may be aided by a rigorous exercise routine and other weight loss practices such as taking laxatives or slimming pills. Not all anorexics are thin, but they usually are, the average weight of an anorexic being 15 per cent below that recommended for the age, height and sex of the person. An abnormally low body weight is generally accompanied by the cessation of menstrual periods (amenorrhoea) in girls.

People diagnosed with Body Dysmorphic Disorder (see Chapter 5) have a distorted view of some aspect of their appearance. It is the same with anorexia – the person believes she is larger than she actually is. A young woman of average looks and emaciated appearance who mistakenly believes she's overweight and of unsightly appearance may be given a diagnosis of both anorexia and Body Dysmorphic Disorder.

Therapists, doctors and other health care professionals are reporting ever increasing numbers of young children with anorexia – one study showed that 80 per cent of girls were restricting their food intake by age 11. Anorexia is a very serious problem; many anorexics starve themselves to death. Studies of severe hospitalized cases show that between 5 and 21 per cent of in-patients with anorexia die. Of these, two-thirds die from the physical effects of starvation and a third from suicide. If you have anorexia and find

17

these figures disturbing, try to remember that eating disorders are common and that many other people share your problem. In reading this book you are taking a great step towards recovery. Learn everything you possibly can about the condition and its treatment and you are halfway there.

You may have heard that full recovery from anorexia is not possible – that it's a case of 'once an anorexic, always an anorexic'. This is not true! Studies have shown that recovery is possible. Indeed, recovery rates as high as 60 to 70 per cent five years after treatment have been reported in some studies. Unfortunately, it is a case of the longer you have had the disorder, the harder recovery is to achieve. Follow-up studies, however, have shown that recovery is possible after as long as 12 years of continuous severe symptoms.

Who gets anorexia?

Anorexia is usually found in Caucasian (white) females, and normally begins in adolescence or early adulthood, the average age of onset being 15 years.

Estimates of prevalence vary. The American Academy of Paediatrics Committee on Adolescence suggests that 0.5 per cent of females are anorexic, whereas other estimates put the figure at anywhere between 1 and 4 per cent. Other studies have suggested that one in every 200 females between the ages of 15 and 18 have anorexia. Furthermore, it is known that 10 to 20 per cent of adolescent and young adult females exhibit some of the clinical symptoms of anorexia, but as the full diagnostic criteria are not met they can't be given a diagnosis.

Boys are not immune to the desire to be thin. In 1997, *Elle* magazine carried out a study of 10 and 11 year old boys and found that 43 per cent in that age-group would prefer to be thinner. In a survey commissioned by the *British Journal of Developmental Psychology*, a third of the boys questioned stated that they need to lose weight and have tried to diet an average of four times. This perhaps shows that body image is becoming important to males, with increasing future risk of eating disorders.

Eating disorders tend to run in families. A person whose mother or sisters had anorexia is 12 times more likely than normal to develop it herself.

Clinical studies have shown anorexia to be more common in higher social classes. However, population studies show an equal distribution throughout all social groups. This would suggest that there is a degree of underdiagnosis and undertreatment of the more socially disadvantaged anorexics.

What causes anorexia?

There are several factors that can predispose a person to developing anorexia. They include genetic predisposition, low self-esteem, poor body image, early problems with feeding, communication difficulties within the family, abuse and other childhood traumas. (See Chapter 1 for advice on improving self-esteem.)

Body image

Researchers are now suggesting that the core disturbance in anorexia is not with eating and food, but with body image. The mania for achieving the fashionable shape and size reaches all corners of western society, and now slender celebrities are interviewed about their strict diets in popular magazines. The message this gives is that anyone can have their willpower and glamorous looks, which is simply not true.

Possible genetic predisposition

Because anorexia tends to exist in family groups, there is the possibility of a genetic component. Researchers are currently trying to isolate a gene that may be responsible, though at present there is no firm evidence to distinguish a genetic link with that of learned eating habits from the example of other family members.

Early problems with feeding

When a mother doesn't know how to feed her child appropriately – perhaps due to psychiatric problems, inclusive of anorexia – she may not be fully aware of her child's feeding requirements. As a result, the child is likely to develop a disordered eating pattern.

If the mother has anorexia, eating when she feels she can allow herself to rather than when she is hungry, the child may grow up copying her. Such poor eating habits are liable to tip over into anorexic behaviour.

Communication difficulties within the family

When family members avoid conflict with each other – maybe due to a domineering parent or a fear of the situation spiralling out of control – children fail to develop the ability to express themselves effectively and to work through problematic emotions. As adults, they are likely to be abnormally afraid of conflict and go out of their way to avoid it. They may be the type of person who makes huge compromises in order to avoid conflict – which, emotionally and psychologically, does them no good at all.

The family environment of a child at risk of developing anorexia may also be as follows:

- The parents may still be demanding conformity of behaviour when their child is at an age when she should be taking a few risks and learning to be independent.
- The parents may be high-achievers and expect the same of their child.
- The parents may not encourage their child to talk about problems.
- Where the daughter is at risk, there may not be a strong relationship between mother and daughter.
- One parent may be involved with the child, while the other is passive or absent.
- There may be intense sibling rivalry.

Abuse

Abuse in childhood can come in the following forms:

- Sexual abuse – i.e. molestation or incest between parent and child or between siblings, or sexual abuse from a relative or family friend.
- Physical abuse – i.e. one or both parents beating or neglecting the child. Physical abuse can come from older siblings, too.
- Emotional abuse – i.e. verbal bullying and constant criticism from parents or siblings.

It is when childhood abuse is not discussed and swept under the carpet that the child becomes more predisposed to developing an eating disorder. Sexual abuse makes the child vulnerable whether or not she has talked about it and had counselling.

Other childhood trauma

It is thought that any kind of trauma can make a child susceptible to developing anorexia. Apart from abuse, trauma can come from the shock of an accident, a life-threatening illness, the sudden loss of a loved one or an episode of severe bullying. When the child feels unable to talk about the trauma to parents or siblings, the negative feelings can become displaced, the child believing her size and weight are the real problem.

How is anorexia triggered?

The condition is generally triggered by the success of a first diet, which brings feelings of achievement and self-control – she may never have experienced such positive feelings about herself. If that first diet doesn't become a habit, a second, third or fourth diet does (see Chapter 1), and the habit turns into the compulsive, obsessive or addictive behaviour that is associated with anorexia.

Typical anorexics have the following personality traits:

- They tend to be high-achievers.
- They tend to set high standards for themselves.
- They are likely to be well-organized and mildly obsessional.
- They tend to be perfectionists, believing that anything less than excellence means failure.
- They can be inflexible in their behaviour.
- They tend to feel insecure in their lives.
- They can feel their lives are out of control.
- They believe the hype that 'thin' is the ideal body shape.

Often the first diet is triggered by a specific event:

- A family argument.
- An argument with a friend.
- A casual remark to the effect that the person is overweight.
- An episode of being teased or bullied – not necessarily about the individual's weight.
- School exams.
- Feelings of being different from her peers.
- Romantic problems, such as the boy wanting too much too soon, the girl not being able to cope with deep emotions, the stress of suspecting the boy of being unfaithful, or the heartache of the boy finishing the relationship. Being let down in love is a common trigger for anorexia. The failure of same-sex relationships is also a trigger.

The anorexic diet

Individuals on a normal diet and anorexics on a diet have the following in common:

- The goal is to lose weight.
- They cut down on food intake.
- They eat diet foods.
- They learn calorific values.
- Exercise may be used to speed up weight loss.

The above are surface similarities between anorexia and normal dieting. The differences between the two are numerous and significant, with anorexics generally behaving as follows:

- They learn calorific values obsessively so they can remember the value of everything they eat without referring to a calorie chart.
- They have tunnel vision about dieting, yet are likely to deny being on a diet or wanting to lose weight.
- They hide their weight loss by wearing baggy clothes. However, in the anorexic's mind, the baggy clothes cover her heaviness, not the fact that she is thin.
- They won't admit to feeling hungry or to craving certain foods – particularly high-calorie foods.
- They feel guilty after eating.
- They cut their food into small pieces to make the meal last longer.
- They take time over eating. An anorexic will eat slowly and try to finish after everyone else.
- They eat less than those around them. For a female anorexic, it is important that she eats less than her mother or sisters.
- They are not disturbed by the nearness of food, but rather the reverse. People with anorexia think of food all the time; many like to do the family food shopping and cook for the family.
- They become gradually averse to eating in front of others. Many anorexics hide food to eat in private.
- They never treat themselves to the odd cream bun, packet of crisps, bar of chocolate and so on. If they let their resolve drop for a moment, they secretly despise themselves afterwards and are very upset.
- They are preoccupied with the thought that their bodies are too heavy and by the desire to be slim.
- They see a distorted image of themselves. While a girl grows ever

more thin, she sees someone who is grossly overweight in the mirror.

- They develop obsessive behaviour in the presence of food. For instance, a young man may feel compelled to tap the handle of the knife on the table three times before each mouthful of food.
- They may start following certain rituals. For instance, a girl may feel she needs to touch the living room doorknob seven times an hour to stop her mother from dying in an accident.
- When they exercise, they concentrate on the calories they are burning up.

If you can identify with the majority of the above, or if your daughter, son, friend, etc. is displaying much of this type of behaviour, there can be little doubt that anorexia is the cause. Read on and you will learn more. You can then start to prise apart the bars of the cage in which you or the person affected is trapped.

What is it like to be anorexic?

People with anorexia have an intense fear of being overweight, yet see themselves as gross. They diet madly to lose weight, eliminate red meat and limit themselves to small amounts of white meat and non-oily fish. They also cut out other high-fat foods such as cheese, eggs, butter, cream, margarine, bread, cakes, sweets, desserts, sugary cereals and mayonnaise. When anyone challenges them about the inadequacy of their diet, they say they know a lot about nutrition and are eating healthily by cutting out the bad things. What they do eat is usually small helpings of low-calorie foods such as vegetables, fruits, salads with non-oily dressings, cottage cheese and low-fat yoghurt.

An obsession with food

Although anorexics eat very little, they are obsessed with food and enjoy working with it. They are likely to read recipe books, do the food shopping and cook for the family or friends. However, despite their great interest in food, they employ enormous willpower to keep their own food intake low, and are proud of their self-control.

Bulimic behaviour

Every now and again, some anorexics give in to their ravenous hunger and indulge in a binge-eating session that leaves them feeling guilty and afraid. Their only answer, as they see it, is to vomit the food back up as would a bulimic, then return to their anorexic behaviour. There are many anorexics who regularly binge and purge, just as there are many others who keep strictly to their self-imposed rules.

As well as self-induced vomiting after bingeing, people with anorexia may use laxatives or diuretics (tablets that rid the body of fluids). The psychological, physiological and biochemical effects of such actions are as follows:

- *Psychological*. Violent mood swings, anxiety, depression, feelings of isolation and lowering of self-esteem.
- *Physiological*. Dilation of the small intestine which produces a bloated feeling. Existing constipation is worsened.
- *Biochemical*. Dehydration due to reduced levels of potassium and chloride in the blood. This can cause lethargy and muscular weakness, tingling in the hands and feet and, if severe, heart irregularities.

Keeping active

Many anorexics try to stay on the move. They start walking to school or work instead of driving or accepting a lift, and they volunteer to fetch things so they have to dash about and climb the stairs. They also use bouts of strenuous physical exercise as a weapon against weight gain, working out until they feel that the calories they consumed have all been burnt off. Sitting still and relaxing is foreign to them. In fact, when they have to wait a long time in a queue, for example, they can become extremely agitated and imagine calories converting to fat. Physical activity is soon dominating their day, and they find any periods of enforced inactivity traumatic.

Changes in thinking

People with anorexia see the world in a different way from everyone else. Their sense of identity is dependent on the narrowest of factors, namely their ability to control their food intake and weight – they feel good about the former, but very bad about the latter, for they feel perpetually overweight.

Starvation point

When an anorexic reaches starvation point, she enters an altered state of consciousness – becoming 'punch drunk'. Her thinking is slower, her short-term memory very poor and her speech becomes slow and rather slurred. These things are accompanied by anxiety, poor concentration, indecisiveness, emotional instability, social withdrawal and lack of libido. (It should be said that anorexics avoid sexual relations anyway because of their poor opinion of their bodies.)

Obsessions, compulsions and addictions

A person with anorexia is likely to behave in an obsessive, compulsive or addictive manner at times. It may begin with being obsessively neat, tidy, clean and punctual and turn into obsessive behaviour around food. This may include thoughts such as 'If I eat a baked potato with cottage cheese this evening, I can't let one piece of food pass my lips for at least 18 hours'; or 'For every mouthful I swallow, I have to do ten sit-ups and ten minutes on my exercise bike.' Moreover, a particular part of the body may start to receive obsessive attention, like the ankles or wrists, which may be measured over and over to work out the imagined fat gained or lost.

As the anorexia progresses, time-consuming rituals that are both compulsive and addictive are likely to arise. These often start as a means of keeping activity levels high and to divert attention from the physical discomfort of hunger. The rituals are each as unique as the person who conceives and implements them, and may include taking a shower after every meal, tapping the doorknob five times on going out of the room and touching each wall of the bedroom eight times before getting into bed.

Some anorexics excuse themselves from their obsessional rules and impose them on other people instead. This can make them extremely intolerant of people who are untidy, unpunctual and so on. Ultimately, they feel unable to cope with anyone who doesn't cater to their obsessions, and this makes them more isolated and alone. It also makes the people around them feel more frustrated and helpless.

Stereotyped thinking

Anorexics may repeat certain phrases over and over, like a chant. This prevents them from progressing from one thought or idea to another; it makes them unable to develop ideas, opinions and defences. People who argue with anorexics say it is like going around in circles.

Social withdrawal

All in all, it's difficult for individuals with anorexia to be around other people. They may find it almost impossible to see the other's point of view. If advice is given, the anorexic rejects it immediately and feels very defensive. They assume that anyone who tells them they're too thin is wrong and has a distorted view of the anorexic's appearance. In time, someone with anorexia may cease taking phone calls, refuse to see friends, and stop going out of the house. Some don't bother getting dressed at this stage, neither may they shower nor clean their teeth – and because they are afraid of feeling the imagined fat on their bodies, they try to avoid touching their naked flesh. Moreover, their imagined weight may stop them from looking in mirrors.

Depression

It is common for people with anorexia to develop depression, and for depressive symptoms to become more pronounced as more weight drops off. The depression of anorexia can make the person feel empty or dead inside. Persistent low mood, lack of energy, poor sleep, poor memory and concentration and feelings of guilt and worthlessness are usually experienced. Furthermore, anorexics tend to have a negative view of themselves and the world around them.

The physical effects of anorexia

There are some serious and sometimes potentially fatal physical complications that come with anorexia. My aim, in writing about them, is not to frighten you but only to inform you so that you can take measures towards change – physical complications can be reversed, or their progress halted. Frightening sufferers has proven ineffective as a means of changing their behaviour. Indeed, some anorexics have made the informed decision that they prefer to be very thin and risk serious complications than be overweight.

Appearance

As an anorexic loses more and more weight, her face and body take on an emaciated appearance and her bones start to protrude. Her skin becomes dry and tough and fine body hair called lanugo grows. Also, her skin takes on a yellowish tinge, her palms turn quite orange, her lips become broken and cracked and her hair becomes dry and much of it falls out.

These changes can all reverse, however, once she gains body weight and her systems are running more efficiently again.

Metabolism

When the body is undernourished, as in anorexia, weight loss slows down. The body adapts to what it imagines are 'famine conditions' by slowing the metabolism and burning calories at a slower pace. As a result, the person's growth rate is restricted, causing late onset of puberty in pre-pubescent children and often stopping periods in girls and women of menstruating age. Combined with the loss of essential body fat, the individual feels cold far more acutely at this stage, even becoming hypothermic at times.

When extreme feelings of fatigue and weakness occur, the starved body is attempting to make the individual reduce activity levels and thus conserve energy. However, the anorexic's all-consuming need to be active generally overrides even this. The feeling many anorexics experience at this stage – that they are at war with their bodies – is the body actually shouting out to the brain that it needs food and rest.

If starvation continues, the brain's regulatory systems are over-ridden and epileptic fits can occur. Unfortunately, these are not uncommon in anorexia. However, all metabolic problems are restored to normal when weight is gained and a proper eating pattern formed.

Mineral deficiencies

The body can become deficient in essential minerals, causing weak muscles and low back pain. A lack of calcium can lead to the development of osteopenia, where bone mineral density is lost. The more serious osteoporosis – a disease where the bones are weakened and liable to break – is also capable of developing. In fact, in a 2000 Massachusetts study, a group of anorexic women in their mid-twenties were tested for osteopenia and 92 per cent were found to have it in their spine or hips. Of these, 25 per cent also had osteoporosis in the spine and 16 per cent had osteoporosis in the hip.

A deficiency in potassium can lead to heart problems, for potassium helps to regulate the heartbeat. On the other hand, a lack of sodium can cause dangerously low blood pressure and severe dehydration.

Mineral deficiencies will revert to normal once weight is gained. Osteopenia and osteoporosis are permanent conditions, however. It is the progression of these diseases that is halted when normal eating resumes.

Muscle weakness

When food intake is severely reduced, the body turns to its fat reserves for nourishment. In anorexia, when the fat reserves are used up, the body will make use of what little food it gets, then begins to break down the muscles for fuel. In extreme cases, this can even include heart muscle, causing it to be less efficient at pumping blood around the body. Moreover, the individual is likely to take on the appearance of a much older, more haggard person whose muscles are wasting due to old age. Climbing stairs can be difficult, as can getting up from a squatting position and doing any lifting.

The state of the muscles will slowly return to normal once the person is eating proper meals.

Kidney function

The starvation that comes with anorexia can cause blood pressure to be low, and this can result in poor kidney function. Persistent dehydration – where the body is short of water, as occurs in starvation – will eventually damage the kidneys.

Kidney damage is generally irreversible, but blood pressure and dehydration should normalize when weight gain takes place.

Gastro-intestinal problems

When a body is starved, the whole of the gastro-intestinal tract, from the throat to the rectum, will shrink. As a result, the person will have the feeling of being full when only small amounts of food and drink have been consumed. The poor enzyme activity caused by starvation also means that of the little food eaten, not all is absorbed into the system correctly.

Constipation is another common problem in anorexia. It can give rise to severe abdominal pain as well as discomfort on going to the toilet. 'Faecal impaction' is likely to occur, too, in which digested material is trapped in the bowel and cannot be excreted in the normal way. It has to be removed by a doctor or nurse. Constipation problems are often the reason the individual first seeks medical help, and from which anorexia may first be diagnosed.

The gastro-intestinal system should revert to normal once the person starts to eat properly again.

The reproductive system

In girls of reproductive age with anorexia, the uterus and ovaries shrink and periods are liable to cease. In the unlikely event of a pregnancy, there is an increased risk of miscarriage, for the body finds it difficult to sustain two lives. If a pregnancy goes to term and a live birth results, the undernourished baby may be very small and have learning difficulties as it grows.

The immune system

In people who are starving, the ability of the immune system to defend the body against viral and bacterial attack can be impaired. The individual is therefore more likely to catch colds, flu and other infections.

The immune system is fully restored once normal eating resumes.

Excessive exercise

Exercise is of great benefit to health, and has to be encouraged. It is when exercise is excessive and used as a tool to lose the calories consumed that the person can run into trouble. For instance, too much exercise can cause problems within the nervous and endocrine systems, manifested as muscle soreness, fatigue, joint aches, bad skin, dehydration and insomnia.

You should keep a record of how much time you are exercising, then try to limit it to no more than half an hour a day of gentle exercise, such as walking or swimming, which is a healthy amount for anyone. Allow your muscles sufficient time to recover after each session. It is recommended that a person does strenuous exercise for no more than four days out of seven.

When anorexics binge and purge

When the starvation of anorexia is punctuated by bingeing and purging, severe heartburn can arise – this being a burning sensation in the chest. Heartburn is caused by stomach acids forcing themselves up into the gullet (oesophagus) – a situation known as acid reflux. Avoiding milk and milk protein products can ease the pain.

It is common for anorexics who binge and purge to have swelling (odoema) in the fingers and legs, and puffiness in the face. The swelling is caused by the low levels of salt (sodium chloride) that comes with repeated vomiting. The facial puffiness is different from that in bulimia.

Relationships with others

Not only does anorexia affect the mind and body of the individual, it also affects the way others relate to them. Different people can react in different ways:

- When the anorexic is very emaciated someone who hasn't seen them for a while may back off and feel afraid of what they are observing. Face to face, they may not know how to react.
- A person who sees an anorexic on a regular basis may one day act with consideration and another be very firm in trying to convince her to start eating properly. The person may even shout, threaten, and try to argue with her.
- At home, brothers and sisters may be jealous of the attention the person with anorexia is receiving from their parents. They may taunt her in secret and try to make her look bad in front of their parents.
- The anorexic's parents may have different ideas on how to deal with her and end up arguing with each other. If the anorexic is closer to one parent than the other, the other may feel left out. The parent's relationship may deteriorate, with the more distant parent blaming the child with anorexia.
- Some anorexics believe they have to be ill to be taken seriously. They may use their anorexia to get attention from their parents, or even to hurt them.
- Anorexics with partners are likely to have difficulties with sexual relations. This is due to hormonal disturbances and a psychological barrier the sufferer may put up to wall off her emotions. There is also a fear of being naked, a fear of being touched and of touching someone else. As a result, partners can feel unloved and rejected.

Your doctor

If you think you are suffering from anorexia, it is strongly advised that you see your doctor as soon as possible. Depending on the severity of your condition, specialized help at an Eating Disorder Unit may be required (see below).

Medications

Medications called Selective Serotonin Re-uptake Inhibitors (SSRIs) can be used to great effect as part of the treatment package for anorexia, especially if you also suffer from depression and obsessive-compulsive disorder. SSRIs can allow you to become more compliant with the regime necessary for improving your self-esteem and for helping you to eat normally. These drugs also decrease anxiety, panic and social phobia.

In-patient treatment

If you are very underweight, hospital admission may be deemed by your doctor as essential. Initially, the hospital will allow you a time for reflection, for patients are restricted to their rooms and immediate corridor area. During this time, while a correct eating pattern is encouraged, you will get to know the staff and your fellow patients. There is a varied and well-balanced diet, and weight gain will normally be controlled to between 1.0 and 1.5 kilos (2.2 to 3 lbs) per week. People with severe anorexia usually remain on the unit for two weeks, whereas milder cases generally stay for only 72 hours.

When a regular eating pattern is established and your weight reaches a normal healthy range, your underlying feelings will begin to emerge. The remainder of the programme is devoted to helping you to identify and work through these feelings. Cognitive Behavioural Therapy (CBT) – that is, one-to-one discussions with a fully trained and very sensitive therapist – explores some of the mechanisms underlying the thought processes that were leading to your false beliefs and unhealthy behaviours. You will then be shown how to challenge that thinking. Creative therapies, including art therapy and drama therapy, are used as non-verbal means of identifying and understanding your feelings. Body image and assertiveness training are also included in CBT, and you will be shown techniques for exploring and challenging your automatic responses.

Parents are usually asked to take part in family therapy with the patient. During these sessions, family relationships and their communication methods are explored. Direct communication within the family is encouraged, and the family is gently made aware that family relationships may have contributed to the development or perpetuation of your illness.

During CBT and family therapy, you will be given increasing freedom to spend time in other parts of the unit. By the time you are ready to leave the unit, you will be eating in the main hospital dining room unsupervised. Follow-up therapy is given in the months after your departure.

See Chapter 7 for advice on normalizing your eating, improving your self-esteem and many more things. There is also advice in Chapter 1 regarding self-esteem.

3

Bulimia

Like anorexia, bulimia (full name, bulimia nervosa) is a dangerous eating disorder characterized by repeated episodes of overeating and an intense fear of weight gain. 'Bulimia' means 'the hunger of an ox' and relates to the large amounts of food sufferers consume. This binge-eating is followed by an equally compelling need to purge all that food from their bodies. A binge–purge cycle will frequently interrupt a long-term diet, and is usually triggered by emotional stress.

Purging methods vary from self-induced vomiting to the use of various medications, either alone or in combination. They include laxatives, medications that make you vomit (emetics), medications that take fluids from your body (diuretics), as well as enemas and diet pills. All these methods are potentially harmful.

When bulimia is severe, many thousands of calories can be eaten in one session – most typically sugar, fats and 'simple' carbohydrates such as chocolate, ice cream, sweet pastries, cakes, biscuits, puddings and sugary cereals. To prevent the otherwise inevitable consequence of weight gain, there may be periods where very little food is eaten and purging still used. When vomiting is employed as a purgative, binges can be numerous with repeated cycles of eating and vomiting over several hours. The drive to eat can be so powerful that bulimics may scavenge leftovers from a dustbin or steal from a friend or relative's home. As a rule, bulimics find their behaviour disgusting and are deeply ashamed. They therefore carry out their behaviour in utmost secrecy.

The hunger of a bulimic is almost always driven by her emotions, a binge giving an initial 'rush' or a feeling of letting go of pressures and problems. However, bingeing and purging may make her feel quite out of control. Bulimia may also result in out of control behaviour in other areas, and can be linked with shoplifting, alcoholism, drug abuse or inappropriate sexual activity.

The first vomit may occur almost by accident as a means of getting rid of the full feeling that is normal after eating a good meal – and the subsequent emptiness can create a 'high' that becomes addictive. Before long, self-induced vomiting is so automatic and habitual that the person finds it difficult to keep food in her stomach.

However, during the binge process, some food will be absorbed into her system, and this is generally adequate to ensure a slim appearance without triggering alarm bells in others. When laxatives are used, the individual starts with a few tablets, increasing to massive quantities as the bowel muscles become less able to function. The pain experienced from laxative abuse is usually seen by the person as self-punishment for indulging in such a shameful habit.

Someone who is addicted to binge-eating and purging may look fairly normal – this is the reason many cases go unnoticed until health problems arise. However, bulimia is a harmful illness and its medical complications can be fatal in some cases.

The main characteristics of bulimia are as follows:

- Recurring episodes of bingeing – eating large quantities of food in a short space of time (less than two hours).
- A feeling of lack of control over how much is being eaten.
- Shame and self-disgust due to overeating and purging.
- An intense fear of weight gain.
- A binge–purge cycle that occurs at least twice a week for three months or more. This is the main diagnostic criterion.

Going on one diet after another (yo-yo dieting) causes weight gain rather than loss in the long-term. As a result, the individual feels a failure and a little more of her self-esteem is sheared away, not to mention the further damage to her body image. Dieters can be likened to tightly wound springs – the more restrained their eating the tighter the spring is wound. When suddenly a person feels compelled to eat, the spring releases – and those on a most restrictive diet experience the most forceful release, the greater binge.

It is the constraints of the diet and the inability of the person to follow it without 'letting go' that are the prime factors in the onset of the binge–purge behaviour of bulimia.

Who gets bulimia?

It is estimated that 2 per cent of the female population suffer from bulimia. If we include people in the early stages of the disorder or who are partially recovered, that figure can probably be doubled. The percentage of females versus males with bulimia has not yet been established, but it is estimated that males constitute 10 to 20 per cent of bulimic patients in the western world.

Studies have shown that, sadly, bulimia is now stealing into the pre-teen age group with children as young as 11 using vomiting as a weight-loss technique. However, bulimia usually surfaces at 16 to 18 years of age. At this time, the person may be in the process of separating emotionally, and maybe even physically, from home. If she is working and living away from home, she is likely to be able to find the money for large amounts of food and the time alone in which to indulge in the habits of bulimia.

It is increasingly common for people in their 20s and 30s to develop the condition.

What causes bulimia?

Bulimia is fairly common in western society and, like other eating disorders, can largely be attributed to the constant bombardment of powerful media images that glorify thinness. In fact, eating disorders only occur in the West where looks are everything. Female ballet dancers, fashion models and athletes are the most vulnerable of all – however, most of us have a strong desire to be slim.

Bulimia is known to run in families, especially on the female side. Indeed, a girl is four times more likely to develop it if her mother and sisters had it at some point. Many of the factors that predispose a person to developing bulimia are the same as those for anorexia. This section is, therefore, in brief.

People at risk of developing bulimia tend to have the following character traits and background:

- They are low in confidence, unassertive, have a poor body image and low self-esteem.
- They tend to be perfectionists, always striving to be well-presented and the best in every way.
- They may be intelligent, articulate and socially competent.
- They have a need to please others.
- They are likely to be easily influenced by the media.
- They may have difficulty dealing with conflict and communicating negative emotions.
- They may find it difficult to express anger.
- They may have a fear of the physical changes that come with puberty.

- They may have a troubled family background such as arguments between parents, the absence of one parent, or parental under- or overinvolvement.
- They may have been physically, emotionally or sexually abused in childhood.
- They may have mood problems, particularly bouts of depression.
- There may have been family issues around eating. Having a mother who constantly diets and is anxious about her weight is a high-risk factor, as is tension at family meals and criticism regarding eating.
- They may have parents who struggled with depression.
- They may have peers with bulimia.
- They may be surrounded by weight-conscious people, at home, work and school.
- They may suffer from other obsessive behaviour.

Bulimia can follow anorexia

It is common for bulimia to develop following an episode of anorexia. After a period of intense dieting, some may lose control and binge on the type of food they had deprived themselves of. The individual is usually terrified by what she has done and, not wanting the food to be digested, sees making herself sick as the only solution. For some people, bingeing and purging is a large part of their anorexia. It is when the binge–purge episodes become numerous and frequent that the condition flips over diagnostically into bulimia. Whether it is anorexia or bulimia that's diagnosed at this point is not too important. What is important is that treatment is sought.

How is bulimia triggered?

As with anorexia, bulimia often starts with a strict weight-loss diet and subsequent feelings of achievement and control. The diet may be the result of a particular trigger, an emotional issue the individual finds deeply upsetting that causes them to displace their emotional problems. They feel their problem is actually their weight and body shape, and that when they reach their ideal weight and shape their other problems will miraculously disappear.

Possible triggers for that first diet include:

- Teasing about being overweight by a peer, despite the individual being well within the 'normal' weight range.

- The sudden end of a romantic relationship.
- The death of someone close.
- Divorce.
- A disappointment.
- An instance of bullying, not necessarily about weight.
- Weight loss after an illness. Flattering comments from others after involuntary weight loss may make the person begin a rigorous diet so the weight stays off.

Bulimia is not always the result of a trigger. The individual may have bulimic school friends from whom the rationale and techniques of bingeing and purging are learned. A weekend habit can thus quickly become full-blown bulimia that is difficult to conquer. Other causes can be as straightforward as boredom and loneliness.

Do you or someone you know suffer from bulimia?

A person with bulimia may be able to keep her weight stable, so weight loss is not always a sign. Her secretive behaviour can also make recognition difficult. Often it is not until associated health problems arise that the problem comes to light.

Here are the signs to watch out for:

- People with bulimia rarely eat around other people.
- They are secretive about their eating.
- Their weight may fluctuate, although not always.
- They may have financial problems due to high spending on food.
- They may suffer from stomach pain due to laxative abuse.
- The person may have an 'ill' appearance, with symptoms such as tooth decay, bleeding gums, dry skin, thin hair and lack of energy.
- There may be puffiness of the face and fingers.
- There may be grazes on forefinger knuckles, where vomiting is used as a purgative and the fingers scrape against the front teeth. Some bulimics have a chronic blister on the forefinger knuckle where it rubs against the upper teeth.
- Repeated vomiting leads to swelling of the salivary glands that show as soft swellings at the base of the ears just under the chin. (Over time, the swellings become hard and permanent.)
- You might notice a lot of laxatives or diuretics in a cupboard or drawer.

- If the person lives at home, large quantities of food may go missing.

How a dieting habit becomes bulimia

In the early days of bulimia, an individual has a compulsion to eat large amounts of food, together with a compulsion to be slim. Obviously these things don't go together, so in between the binges and purges, they stick to a diet, or sometimes avoid food altogether for a period. The body assumes this is 'famine time' and slows down the metabolism in order to conserve energy. If the person attempts to return to her old eating habits, her slow metabolism ensures she gains weight. She may try to diet once more, but more weight is gained soon after the diet ends. The person is very quickly a 'yo-yo dieter', her weight going up a little more between each diet.

The weight gain is loathed and detested, however. The individual hears about purging and either tries it straightaway, or finds herself bingeing and purging after a particular emotional upset, such as an argument with a parent. The 'rush' obtained from vomiting at first offsets any feelings of disgust. With laxative abuse, the knowledge that the binge is literally going 'down the pan' offsets the discomfort of the resulting diarrhoea. The person even manages to ignore the lightheadedness and muscle weakness that accompany laxative abuse.

Bingeing and purging occur on several more occasions, and the physical side-effects become easier to disregard. Feelings of shame and fear are likely to be experienced in each cycle, but the need to repeat it is overwhelming, and so the cycle goes on.

The bingeing is now the focus of the person's life, the purging just a necessary evil. She may make space in her schedule for her binge–purge cycle, but the need will be strongest on days when she feels bored, tense, upset, angry or depressed. Immediately before the binge she may experience anxiety and tension, maybe heart palpitations and sweating. She may not even be hungry, but feels a compulsion to eat lots of starchy, sugary high-fat foods or puddings, ice cream and other milky foods that can easily be vomited. As she starts to binge, she enters a trance-like state and is no longer aware of her body or her surroundings. She tastes barely anything and manages to ignore the painful sensations of a stomach in distress. The binge only ends when she feels exhausted, if she is interrupted, or the pain finally penetrates her consciousness. Then begins the purgative process, either by vomiting, laxative abuse or some other means.

What is it like to be bulimic?

Many of us 'binge-eat' at times – having a whole box of chocolates or our favourite cheese crackers to ourselves. However, this is not bingeing as known in bulimia. It is only in bulimia that the food eaten is disposed of by purging, and it is only in bulimia that both the bingeing and purging run out of control.

Many bulimics prepare secretly for binges, cooking or buying 'unhealthy' food beforehand then hoarding it until required. Others obtain their binge food in the following ways:

- They raid the fridge.
- They prepare simple meals during the time period of the binge.
- They go from café to café eating junk food.
- They go from shop to shop, inclusive of fast-food outlets, buying and eating junk food.

During a binge, the individual will gulp the food quickly, maybe stuffing it frantically into her mouth. If she knows she is not going to be disturbed, she is likely to eat a little more slowly. A binge may occur at any time of the day or night, and the food eaten can be up to 30 times the amount she would consume in one day if she was eating normally. Someone who has recently developed bulimia can abandon themselves to between one and six bingeing sessions in a day. On the other hand, a person who has a long history of bulimia may have the capacity to indulge in up to 20 sessions a day.

The binge will often end because the person simply runs out of steam. Alternatively, she may feel nauseated, be experiencing the discomfort of an overfull stomach, or be about to be discovered. Some bulimics give themselves a time-scale for their binges – a time when they know they will not be disturbed. However, when their time is up, it is generally one of the above factors rather than willpower that stops them eating.

A bulimic binge is terrifying for the individual, for it seems they have no control over their eating. They find the amount they eat disgusting, and experience a strong sense of self-loathing in regard to their compulsion to purge. Feelings of anger, panic, nervousness, loneliness and inadequacy are often also experienced.

Bulimia has a profound effect on the psychological well-being of the individual, for depression and anxiety commonly occur, combined with difficulties in the individual's personal and social life. As with anorexia, the self-esteem of a person with bulimia is related to her perception of her weight and shape – and because she feels these things are unacceptable she feels she is worthless.

Up to two-thirds of people with bulimia suffer from depression, largely because of their inability to control their eating and their concerns about their size and shape. A loss of confidence and withdrawal from social contact run side by side in bulimic depression. It is also common for people with bulimia to feel desperate at times. They loathe what they are doing, they feel good for nothing and thoroughly despise themselves. And because they see no possibility of change in the future, a suicide attempt is always a possibility. Approximately 5 per cent of people with bulimia who seek treatment have taken an overdose of pills in the past.

Are you bulimic?

The following is a list of typical bulimic thoughts and behaviours. Do any of them apply to you?

- I think about food most of the time.
- I love to eat but refuse to put on weight.
- I eat even when I'm not hungry.
- I find it difficult to know when I'm full.
- I hoard food in my room.
- I have used some of the following to control my weight: self-induced vomiting, laxatives, diet pills, diuretics, emetics, enemas and fasting.
- I spend a lot of money each week on junk food.
- When I'm desperate to binge, I consider stealing money or food.
- When I binge, I eat large quantities of food that I don't really taste.
- I binge in private.
- I eat until I'm too exhausted to continue or until it hurts too much to continue.
- I feel uncomfortable about eating in public.

- I deal with stress and tension by bingeing and purging.
- I often feel sad and depressed.

Relationships with others

Because of the shame tied in with their bulimia, many keep their condition a secret for years. In order to do this, they maintain a physical distance from others. However, as they are also hiding away a fundamental part of their emotional selves, they can find themselves emotionally isolated – even when they live with their families.

A person with bulimia will only mix socially when she feels less disturbed than normal about her weight and shape. When she feels heavy, she may withdraw for weeks at a time. At social events, bulimics are afraid they may not be able to control the urge to binge, so are fearful of eating – a problem as much of ordinary social life takes place around eating. Bulimics are also afraid they may not be able to control the need to purge afterwards, even when eating has not been part of a binge. Of course, when others know that a person is inclined to vomit back her food, they are reluctant to ask her out for a meal anyway! Many bulimics feel like outcasts and live isolated lives, and of course the bulimia then worsens, for it is used to cope with the pain of isolation.

Whether a bulimic lives with her parents or alone, the bathrooms may start to smell and the toilets may never be completely clean. Furthermore, her bed linen may be soiled due to constant diarrhoea or the use of a receptacle for vomit in bed. If she goes so far as to steal money from her family and friends to support her addiction, these people may lose their sympathy altogether and instead feel very angry towards her.

At this point, the situation can become intensely harrowing, with family in particular taking a 'hard line'. If the individual firmly refuses to change, her family may shout at her, try to shame her, even ask her to leave home. A person with bulimia is not generally painfully thin, unlike a person with anorexia. Bulimics therefore receive tougher treatment – but what the people around her often don't understand is that it is difficult to change without specialized treatment. They forget that this is not about the missing food and money, the awful smell in the bathroom, that instead it's about the individual's struggle with an addictive psychological illness.

However, recovery is possible, if the person wants to be better. The road to recovery is often punctuated with setbacks, but with the right professional help, slow steps can be made towards freedom. And once they are able to socialize freely, the lives of recovering bulimics are truly transformed. The end of mood swings, depression and anxiety have happy repercussions on intimate and personal relationships, and life vastly improves.

The physical and emotional effects of bulimia

It is not uncommon for someone with bulimia to struggle with one or two further emotional, physical or behavioural problems. For example, 71 per cent of bulimic females have some kind of anxiety disorder. Of those 59 per cent have social phobia and a third have symptoms that worsen in winter, with the onset of Seasonal Affective Disorder. Others will slide into shoplifting, alcoholism, drug abuse or inappropriate sexual activity. It is also estimated that between 50 and 60 per cent of bulimic females suffer from depression.

Apart from eroded tooth enamel and lumps beneath the glands, the damage caused by bulimia can usually be reversed when the person eats normally once more.

The menstrual cycle

A low body weight can cause the periods to become irregular or stop altogether, meaning the chances of conception at this time are poor – a female must have a certain proportion of fat (about 20 per cent) for normal menstruation. Studies have found that a woman needs to be only 5 to 10 per cent beneath her ideal body weight for subtle changes in the menstrual cycle to occur, and this can lead to infertility. Fertility should return once normal eating resumes.

Depression

Many psychological disorders involve some aspect of depression – the general suffering that accompanies illness or stress. A person with depression has a persistent low mood and feels unable to make a difference to anyone any more. She feels dead inside, very lethargic, has poor memory and concentration and feels guilty and worthless. All in all, her view of herself and the world around her is very negative indeed.

Anxiety

Many people with bulimia report that they constantly worry and have anxious forebodings, accompanied by sweating, palpitations, difficulty in breathing and churning in the stomach. The worrying is usually related to concerns about food and their weight and shape. When the eating disorder is brought under control, the anxiety will almost certainly disappear.

Repeated vomiting

Repeated vomiting can cause dehydration and as the acid in the vomit eats into tooth enamel, permanent damage to the teeth can result. Stomach acid – a component of the vomit – can burn the oesophagus, causing scar tissue to form and sores in the mouth. Another possible health problem is known as 'alkalosis', where chemical changes in the body lead to calcium loss. Alkalosis is characterized by tingling in the fingers, muscle spasms in various parts of the body and eventually damage to the heart, lungs and liver. In extreme instances, repeated vomiting can even cause the stomach to rupture.

Fortunately, few people reach the stage where serious damage to the organs occurs or where the stomach is in danger of rupturing. All other damage from repeated vomiting, barring damage to tooth enamel, can be reversed when normal eating resumes.

Misuse of laxatives

Some individuals find it difficult to make themselves sick, so turn to laxatives instead. However, repeated laxative abuse can upset the normal mechanism of the digestive system so it becomes necessary to use laxatives to pass a stool. Laxative abuse can cause constant diarrhoea and rectal bleeding. It can also deplete sodium and potassium levels in the body (as do diuretics), which can give rise to an irregular heartbeat. In some cases, heart failure can occur. Furthermore, laxative abuse can cause failure of some important nutrients to be absorbed into the body, leading to nutritional deficiencies. Once bulimia is conquered, it can take many months or even years for the digestive system to function normally again. In some cases, there may always be problems. Nutritional deficiencies should resolve themselves quite quickly, however.

What many bulimics don't realize is that laxatives are wholly ineffective as a weight-loss technique, for most calories are absorbed from further up the digestive tract. The weight reduction seen on weighing scales after laxatives have been used is the result only of fluid loss, the fluids being a part of the diarrhoea. This is a temporary effect as the person inevitably gets thirsty and has a drink, which restores the fluid balance and returns the body weight to what it was previously.

Misuse of diuretics

Diuretics are pills designed to encourage urination and so reduce the water content in the body. As with laxative abuse, taking diuretics can have no real effect on body weight because when the person takes a drink, her fluid balance returns to what it had been.

The misuse of diuretics can lead to painful swelling throughout the body, which may make the person think she is fat. The swelling is particularly noticeable in the fingers of girls and young women. Reduced levels of potassium in the body can make the legs ache and throb, and feel very weak on walking. These problems disappear, however, once normal eating habits are re-established.

Misuse of emetics

Emetics are pills that cause vomiting, so may be used by people with bulimia in order to lose weight. However, they work by introducing poison to the stomach, which is why they make a person be sick – but repeatedly putting poison in the stomach causes much of it to be absorbed into the system and can be a contributing factor in heart attacks and strokes.

When the person stops using emetics, the risk of a heart attack or stroke is considerably reduced.

Use of diet pills

Drugs which suppress the appetite can produce unwanted side-effects such as chest pain, decreased ability to exercise, fainting, swelling of the feet or lower legs and trouble with breathing. Serious heart or lung problems can arise after extreme misuse. These problems gradually resolve themselves once the person stops taking diet pills.

Your doctor

Currently, the most successful treatment for bulimia is Cognitive Behavioural Therapy (CBT) as described in Chapter 7. Your doctor will make an initial diagnosis and discuss treatment options with you. People with bulimia are usually desperate for help and to be normal again. Therefore, they generally respond well to treatment.

Go to Chapter 7 for advice on normalizing your eating, improving self-esteem and many more things. See Chapter 1 also for advice on raising your self-esteem.

4

Compulsive Eating

In the United States, it is estimated that more than 30 per cent of the population are overweight – that is, their body weight is greater than the given parameters for average weight. In the United Kingdom, estimates are slowly creeping towards that figure, with other western countries following closely behind. It is often said that obesity is of epidemic proportions. These figures would seem to support that.

However, not every overweight person suffers from compulsive eating disorder (sometimes called Binge Eating Disorder). In western society, the main reason for weight gain is the tendency to eat junk food, and to nibble on chocolate bars, biscuits and crisps.

Of course, body type, metabolic rate and body chemistry can also conspire to make an individual prone to putting on weight. People are not doomed to be overweight, however. Those with large frames still have the option of eating in moderation, choosing a variety of high-fibre, low-fat foods and taking a reasonable amount of exercise. This should enable them to be the right weight for their build. The slow metabolism – and hence weight gain – caused by hypothyroidism can be normalized by drugs.

Compulsive eating is characterized by the obsessive consumption and digestion of calories significantly beyond the person's metabolic needs – it is bulimia without the purging, in effect. Individuals who eat such amounts are addicted to food, much as alcoholics are addicted to drink and smokers are addicted to cigarettes. This emotional reliance on an external factor makes the individual feel good at the time of doing and is known as co-dependency.

Two thousand years ago, the philosopher Cicero said, 'We should eat to live, not live to eat'. Compulsive eaters would love to live by this edict, but simply cannot. They feel helpless in the presence of food. Their behaviour is ruled by appetite and desire, not hunger – at least not biological hunger. People who eat compulsively do so in an effort to make their problems go away. A problem rarely goes away for long, however – and its re-emergence only goes to make the person binge-eat once more. Therefore, compulsive eating can also be defined as using food for reasons other than hunger (or bringing hunger to satiation). It is just as much an eating disorder as anorexia and bulimia.

As in bulimia, a compulsive eater will decide to diet as a way of shedding extra pounds and so of feeling better. However, it is the restraint of the diet, the act of denying herself of something she loves that causes her to binge and then to hate herself. A diet-binge-self-contempt cycle is therefore born, and it can last a lifetime if not tackled effectively.

The initial urge to lose weight is usually triggered by today's image of the ideal body, by the feeling of dissatisfaction it engenders and by awareness of the public's prejudice towards overweight people. Dieting seldom makes a person happy, however. All it does is stir feelings of failure when the weight comes back on. It can also cause the pain of an eating disorder.

What causes compulsive eating?

Compulsive eating can develop in childhood when eating patterns are formed. Many compulsive eaters never learned the proper way to deal with stressful situations and used food instead as a means of coping. Some will remember that when they were upset about something, they were given chocolate bars by their mother – and as a result felt comforted. Others will have seen their parents eat chocolate bars or other sweet, high-fat foods to make themselves feel better, and children learn by example. In adulthood, compulsive eaters will then use the same types of foods instead of facing their problems and working them through.

Of course, compulsive eating will cause the weight to pile on. The person responds by going on a diet – after all, it's virtually a sin to be overweight in today's society. Restriction results in a tightening of the spring, and once a problem triggers a binge, the force of the spring letting go is in relation to the severity of restriction – i.e. the stricter the diet, the greater the binge.

Individuals within one family

Various members of one family perhaps use food in different ways to deal with problems. Whether this develops into anorexia, bulimia or compulsive eating depends on the following:

- Their individual personalities.
- The style of parenting. In other words, much depends on the way family members relate to each other, any lack of encouragement to talk about problems, and any pressure to diet or stop dieting.

- External factors such as bullying, a trauma such as sexual, physical or emotional abuse or anything that may contribute to a lack of self-esteem.

The most common causes

There is no doubt that the common denominator in all eating disorders is the presence of low self-esteem, and compulsive eating is no exception. Compulsive eaters focus on their weight and shape instead of attempting to work through painful emotional problems. They may see this new focus as providing an answer to their emotional problems, for giving themselves food can equate to giving themselves love.

Other reasons for compulsive eating are as follows:

- To alleviate stress or depression.
- To fill an emotional void.
- To use food as a tranquillizer. The diet of most compulsive eaters is high in carbohydrates, which have a sedating effect.
- To satisfy the need for instant gratification.
- To protect themselves from intimacy, and as a barrier from the world. This may be unconscious and is particularly common in survivors of sexual abuse.

Emotional issues

It is believed that the majority of compulsive eaters have deep-seated emotional issues, of which they may not even be aware. They use food and eating as a way of hiding from their emotions, to fill a void inside. These emotional issues can come in the following forms:

- Hunger for love.
- A sense of loneliness, or emptiness.
- Disappointment in relationships.
- Negative feelings about themselves, their lives and everyone in it.
- Denial of something.

Hiding from society

Compulsive eaters are generally overweight. Some consciously hide behind their physical appearance, using it as a kind of barricade against society. However, this is only possible because people today tend to idealize slimness and have prejudice against weight. When an individual is carrying excess weight, it is the excess weight that is seen, not the problems going on beneath the surface. A person with emotional problems can, therefore, expect to be more invisible as human beings to others when they are carrying excess weight. It was Wallis Simpson, mistress of Edward VIII who said, 'You can never be too rich or too thin'. Unfortunately, today's society has adopted this phrase as its motto, and for people with underlying emotional issues the excess weight in itself can seem to be the issue. As a result, the individual feels intense shame and guilt for failing to control her weight and bingeing is employed to forget emotional pain – a Catch 22 situation, for it is the weight the binges cause that creates more pain.

If the emotional problems behind the condition are not dealt with, the dieting and bingeing can go on for a lifetime, the person gaining more and more weight.

The health risks of compulsive eating

Recently, the British Medical Council issued the following statement:

> We are unanimous in our belief that obesity is a hazard to health and a detriment to well-being. It is common enough to constitute one of the most important medical and public health problems of our time, whether we judge importance by a shorter expectation of life, increased morbidity, or cost to the community in terms of both money and anxiety.

It is clear that obesity is being taken seriously, but compulsive eating disorder – one cause of obesity – is not. It should be seen as an addiction, a psychological problem, but instead, sufferers are sent only to nutritionists who may put them on yet another diet, or pack them off to a health spa where toning tables and seaweed wraps do nothing at all.

Compulsive eaters are at risk of the same physical and medical complications as people who are overweight for other reasons. The health risks include the following:

- Depression.
- Loss of sex drive.
- Constipation.
- Menstrual irregularities (especially infrequent periods) – Overweight women are likely to be infertile, with irregular or heavy

periods. Fertility and menstruation should return to normal once weight is lost.

- Tooth decay – which can be permanent, even when excess weight is lost.
- Excessive sweating.
- Mobility problems.
- Poor circulation.
- Leg and joint pain.
- Fatigue.
- Heartburn.
- Toxaemia during pregnancy.
- Hypertension (high blood pressure). Weight loss is associated with reduced blood pressure.
- Shortness of breath.
- Varicose veins – this problem may not resolve completely once the excess weight is lost, but the affected veins will be far less painful.
- Hiatus hernia – again, this problem may not resolve completely once excess weight is lost, but it will occur far less often.
- Gall bladder disease – difficult to treat, even when excess weight is lost.
- Sciatica – this stabbing nerve pain, caused by excess weight on the back and legs, usually resolves when excess weight is lost.
- Osteoarthritis, especially of the hips, knees and back. Weight loss will not diminish the disease, but is more effective than drugs at relieving pain.
- Diabetes (type 2) – this disease is five times more common among overweight people. Type 2 diabetes can often be controlled by diet, inclusive of weight loss.
- High cholesterol levels – levels often return to normal when excess weight is lost.
- Liver and kidney disease – these are permanent conditions.
- Heart disease – there is less chance of a heart attack once excess weight is lost.
- Stroke – this is twice as common in overweight people. The risk is no more than normal, however, once weight is within the normal range for sex, height and build.
- Pulmonary embolism – a pulmonary embolism is the name given to a blood clot that lodges in one of the blood vessels that supplies the lungs with blood. It is a very serious condition, and one that can cause death within hours if not medically treated. The chances

of pulmonary embolism occurring are reduced when excess weight is lost.

When a person loses weight so that her Body Mass Index is less than 28, or she falls within the normal range for her sex, height and build, the following should normalize: depression, sex drive, constipation, sweating, mobility, circulation, fatigue, heartburn and shortness of breath.

A reduction in blood pressure and cholesterol levels means that circulation and cardiac (heart) function are improved. There is also an increase in energy, raised self-esteem, improved body image and more confident sexual relationships. Leg and joint pain can disappear when weight is lost, and there is less pain from osteoarthritis and strained muscles in the lower back.

Are you a compulsive eater?

People with a compulsion to overeat feel an inner pressure to act against their own judgement. They experience a regular overwhelming urge to eat irrationally, about which they may or may not be in denial. If you are reading this, you are likely to be at least trying to face up to your problems with eating. It may help for you to determine for certain whether or not you are a compulsive eater. The following signs and symptoms should make things clearer:

- Do you think about food all the time?
- Do you not actually enjoy what you are eating?
- Do you eat very fast, barely chewing your food?
- Do you become anxious while you are eating?
- Do you experience feelings of guilt as you eat?
- Do you continue to eat even after you feel full?
- Do you binge-eat?
- Do you find it impossible to exercise voluntary control over your eating?
- Do you hate yourself after bingeing?
- Do you feel tormented by your eating habits?
- Are you afraid of not being able to stop eating voluntarily?
- Do you suffer from mood swings and depression?
- Do you find it difficult to sleep?
- Are you very unhappy about your body image?

- Is your weight the main focus in your life?
- Are the feelings you have about yourself based on your weight?
- Do you hide food and eat it in secret?
- Do you eat little in public?
- Do you lie to others about how much you eat?
- Do you make self-defeating statements after eating, such as 'I'll never lose any weight' or 'I must be the most useless person in the world'?
- Do you blame any failures socially and professionally on your weight?
- Do you have feelings of rejection or discrimination?
- Do you go on and off diets all the time?
- Do you binge after coming off a diet?
- Do you seem to constantly gain, lose and regain weight?
- Does hunger make you feel uneasy and vulnerable?
- Do you tend to use food like a drug, as a way of coping with problems?
- Do you hold a belief that your weight problems will one day be solved by a new kind of pill or potion?
- Do you trawl the Internet searching for that pill or potion?

If you can identify with about a quarter of the above and don't engage in purging methods after eating, you are probably a compulsive eater. However, the very fact that you are reading this book says you want to conquer the addiction. You should congratulate yourself for taking an important step towards being in control of your diet, rather than your diet being in control of you.

Ruling out other medical factors

It is important that you don't rely completely on self-diagnosis and forgo seeing your doctor. You are strongly recommended to request a thorough medical evaluation, as treatable metabolic disorders such as an underactive thyroid gland can also cause weight gain.

It should be said that it is also possible to be a compulsive eater and, at the same time, suffer from a metabolic disorder. Note, though, that other medical factors – 'gland' problems for instance – are no longer thought to be the principal problem for some overweight individuals. The principal problem is always their relationship with food.

What is it like to be a compulsive eater?

In many developing countries, individuals who are heavier than most are perceived as having high status and are treated with reverence. It is only in the West that excess weight is reviled, overweight children being seen as lazy, greedy, stupid and smelly. Overweight adolescents and adults are discriminated against when it comes to friendships, romance and employment. Being overweight can, therefore, be emotionally and psychologically crippling, causing depression, low moods, poor self-esteem and even self-hatred. One study, included in *The State of the Nation* by the Association of Qualitative Research, has even suggested that obese people feel that society is becoming more hostile to them, with prejudice developing in schools because of the increased number of overweight young people. The study into 'obesity through the eyes of the obese' by Heather Pollitt of ICM Research, concludes that one way of tackling the problem would be for obesity to be reclassified as an illness, and for people to understand that it's a type of addiction, not greed or laziness. Society should then 'spend time thinking about how we can help the sufferers instead of humiliating them'.

It is difficult to know that you are locked into a cycle of behaviour that is causing you to hate the way you look. It is even more difficult when others may believe you are overweight out of greed or feel that you are lazy. Unfortunately, it is society's disdain for people who are overweight and the individual's craving for acceptance that often propels her to follow diet after diet, only to break it each time with an episode of binge-eating. However, the pleasure obtained by eating is very short-lived, for the person is soon furious with herself and will repeat a phrase – a mantra – in her head. It could be 'I'm so fat', or 'I'm good for nothing', or 'I've got absolutely no willpower' or 'I'll never lose weight'. If the mantra is said often enough, the person will believe it to be true and unshakable, hence her subsequent diets will fail.

In today's society, compulsive eating is not yet taken seriously enough. Individuals may be given diet sheets, sent to a health spa or just told sharply to lose weight, to no avail. However, compulsive eating is, like anorexia and bulimia, a serious problem that can result in death. With the proper treatment – this should include nutrition therapy, physical education, and Cognitive Behavioural Therapy – it can be overcome.

It must be said, though, that many compulsive eaters, despite inner turmoil, live fairly good lives. They may eat massive amounts of food every day and be very overweight, but they often have interesting and fulfilling jobs, loving husbands and beautiful children. They also often have respected positions within their communities and many good friends.

Seeing your doctor

It is important that someone with compulsive eating disorder sees their doctor – not only to rule out other weight-gaining conditions, but also to seek advice on available treatments.

Cognitive Behavioural Therapy can help to determine what triggers the overeating response. It can also help to improve self-esteem, tackle negative thinking and give you the confidence and tools to face and deal with any problems you have. A weight control programme will focus on how and for what purpose you use food; it will teach you to differentiate food hunger from emotional hunger, and you will be encouraged to eat small meals regularly throughout the day.

If these treatments are not available to you, or you would prefer to try to tackle the problem yourself first of all, you may find a way out in Chapter 7.

Exercise

Food consumption creates energy within us. When that energy is used for fuelling the body and for taking exercise, there is less left over to convert to fat. It is essential, therefore, that you exercise regularly – especially during a weight loss programme. Exercise can speed up weight loss, whereas a lack of exercise can hinder it.

Some of you may have been inactive for a long period, which will have caused your body to be deconditioned. You may even suffer with low back pain or osteoarthritis. Exercise of some kind is the only real way out of this state of affairs, I'm afraid. It will loosen your joints, condition your muscles and, as you lose weight, reduce any pain. Exercise also prompts the release of endorphins, the 'feel good' chemicals that are capable of reducing the anxiety and depression that can be a part of compulsive eating.

Aerobic activity
Aerobic exercise can be defined as any activity that makes you slightly out of breath. It encourages weight loss and aids overall

fitness. Try to choose an activity you will enjoy and want to continue, for it is important that aerobic activity becomes a part of your everyday life.

You should check with your doctor before embarking on regular aerobic activity.

- *Walking* This most convenient low-impact aerobic activity aids mobility, strength and stamina, and helps to protect against osteoporosis. You may find it easier to use a treadmill, reading a book or magazine at the same time or listening to a walkman, CD player, the radio, or to audio (story) tapes. Aim to walk for 20 or 30 minutes at a time. A treadmill should never wholly replace outdoor walking, however, as fresh air is essential to many of the processes within our bodies.

- *Stepping* Start with a fairly small step (for example, a wide, hefty book, such as a catalogue or a telephone directory), or, if you wish, use a step machine or the bottom step of your staircase. Place first your left foot, then your right foot onto the book or step. Now step backwards, first with your left foot, then with your right. Repeat for 2 to 10 minutes, then change feet, placing first your right foot on the step, then your left.

- *Trampoline jogging* Jogging on a small, circular trampoline can provide a good aerobic workout. If you can manage to get into a rhythm, the trampoline will do much of the work for you. Try to jog in this way for 20 to 30 minutes. Small, inexpensive trampolines are available from most exercise equipment outlets.

- *Aqua aerobics* Many people find aqua aerobics, sometimes called 'aqua-cizes', both easy and enjoyable. Because the water supports your body as you exercise, it removes the shock factor, conditioning your muscles with the minimum of discomfort. The pressure of the water also causes the chest to expand, encouraging deeper breathing and increasing intake of oxygen. Rather than exercising alone in the swimming baths, most people prefer to join an aqua aerobics class. The majority of public swimming baths run aqua aerobic sessions, some of which are graded according to ability. As with all exercises, aqua aerobics are only truly beneficial when performed on a regular basis. If you live a long way from the swimming baths, you will probably find yourself attending less and less, then feel angry with yourself for eventually giving up. To minimize feelings of failure, be wary of undertaking activities that may be difficult to keep up.

- *Swimming* If you enjoy swimming, try to go to the baths once or twice a week and gradually build up the number of lengths you swim. Swimming exercises every muscle in the body in a way that causes them very little stress. However, as with aqua aerobics or visiting a gym, you need to feel sure in yourself, before you start, that you will continue this type of exercise in the long term.
- *Cycling* Whether you use a stationary or ordinary bicycle, this form of activity provides an efficient cardiovascular workout. It is best to start by pedalling slowly and gradually building up momentum – and at first limit your sessions to 2 or 3 minutes, building up to 20 or 30 minutes, if possible.

An exercise routine

Ideally, you should carry out an exercise routine four times a week. If you are not attending Cognitive Behavioural Therapy where exercise is part of the programme, ask your doctor for an exercise sheet. Choose the exercises you feel you can do, then perform three or four repetitions of them four times a week. Start slowly and gently, building up the number of exercises and repetitions when you feel able. Aim to perform ten repetitions of every exercise on the sheet on a long-term basis.

Try to exercise before breakfast, if possible. The low levels of insulin in your body at that time allow access to your body fat for conversion to energy. To boost your fitness levels further – especially if you are unable, as yet, to perform a regular aerobic regime – try walking to work, walking to the shops, getting off the bus a stop or two earlier and taking the stairs instead of the lift. Remember, most of all, that every little helps.

Gradual weight loss

The average weight loss for an overweight person is 2 to 4 kg (4 to 8 lbs) a week in the first few weeks. After that, however, the maximum weight loss may be as little as 0.5 to 1.0 kg (1 to 2 lbs) a week. This is a steady weight loss and, if you can manage it, is fantastic. You should strive to achieve no more than this on a weekly basis. It may take months or even years for you to reach your ideal weight for your sex, height and build, but it will happen eventually.

See Chapter 7 for advice on normalizing your eating, improving self-esteem and many more things. There is advice on raising self-esteem in Chapter 1, as well.

5

Body Dysmorphic Disorder

Body Dysmorphic Disorder (BDD for short) is a psychological condition defined as an obsession with a perceived defect in one's appearance. Many of us are dissatisfied with how we look. We may focus on a particular 'flaw' such as a large nose, bad skin, small breasts, heavy jaw or balding hair – it's the people who are preoccupied excessively who have BDD.

When a defect is present in BDD, an obsessive preoccupation blows it out of all proportion in the individual's mind. Others are likely to not understand the obsession and say, 'Why is she so worried about her looks? I think she's quite pretty', or 'I don't know why he's so bothered about his skin and his nose. He's just a normal-looking guy.' Hearing other people discounting their problems or declaring there's nothing wrong is no help at all to people with BDD. They are suffering from an illness. Their abnormal preoccupation with some aspect of their appearance causes them extreme distress. Furthermore, BDD is likely to interfere with their social life and may even make them afraid of going out to work. Indeed, some are so revolted by their appearance that they hide themselves indoors all the time.

The unusual thing about BDD is that the people who have it focus on defects that others don't see, or consider minimal, so that sufferers are regarded as having a delusion – in fact, the condition is sometimes referred to as 'Imagined Ugliness Syndrome'. Sadly, the 'ugliness' is very real to the person concerned.

People with BDD find it difficult to control their preoccupation with their 'defect' and spend several hours a day thinking about it. In fact, some find it difficult not to think about it, to the point where their preoccupation dominates their lives. People with this condition describe their preoccupation as 'intensely painful', and even 'tormenting'.

The severity of BDD ranges from fairly mild to life-threatening. Some people manage, with great effort, to get on with their lives, whereas others are so stricken they are unable to show themselves, going so far as to wear a concealing mask or hood of some kind when someone insists on seeing them. Such BDDers are likely to be severely depressed, seeing suicide as the only option.

How is BDD defined and diagnosed?

The accepted diagnostic criteria for BDD is as follows:

1. A preoccupation with an imagined defect in appearance. If a slight physical anomaly is present, the person's concern is markedly excessive.
2. The preoccupation causes clinically significant distress or impairment in social, occupational or other important areas of functioning.
3. The preoccupation is not better accounted for by another mental disorder (for example, dissatisfaction with body shape and size as in anorexia nervosa).

Criterion 1 of the definition rules that the defect is either imagined or slight. When 'imagined' the defect is not discernible to others, and when slight it is discernible to others, but within the bounds of what is considered normal, which means it will seldom be noticed. A recent UK study using a scientific measure of facial appearance found that in BDD the focus of dissatisfaction is generally within the normal range.

While some people with BDD realize they're imagining their defect, others are convinced that their way of thinking is correct. It is when the defect is assessable that the diagnosis becomes difficult. Diagnosis of BDD can then only be made if the person's concern is markedly excessive in relation to the defect. If the person has severe acne and cuts down his socializing because of it, it can be said that he does not have BDD. To be diagnosed with BDD, either the acne would need to be mild or the person's behaviour would be extreme in comparison. For example, if he locked himself in his room and went to the extent of wearing a cloth over his head when forced to see a visitor he could be diagnosed with BDD. However, only around 5 per cent of diagnosed BDD cases have an assessable defect.

Where the defect is very obvious – a deformity, for instance – BDD cannot be diagnosed. However, much of the advice in this chapter and Chapter 7 will be of help to such people.

It should also be said that not everyone who is concerned about his or her appearance has BDD. Concern about one's appearance is almost universal in modern society, particularly during adolescence. It is only when concern is 'abnormal' that a diagnosis can be given.

Are anorexia and BDD related?

People with anorexia fall into Criterion 1 for BDD – they have an imagined or slight defect. In other words, they think they're overweight when actually they're thin. The criterion prompts doctors and psychologists to not mix-up the diagnosis. However, researchers are becoming increasingly convinced that anorexia is a disorder of body image and as such is a form of BDD. Currently, one person can receive diagnoses for both anorexia and BDD, but it is uncertain as to whether Criterion 3 will eventually be dropped and people with anorexia be classed as suffering from BDD. There are certainly many people with both conditions.

I recently came across a collection of internet journals made by people with BDD on a website called 'BDD Central' on www.bddcentral.com, and some people had concerns about being overweight when they clearly were not overweight at all. For example, one entry went:

> I had a fairly ok day today. I woke up hating what I saw in the mirror – my blotchy skin and rotund body. Considering I haven't eaten anything since Sunday you'd think I wouldn't feel this way, but I still feel fat. I went to work where it was just like any other day. I repeatedly kept looking at the mirror inside my workstation to make sure nothing had worsened since the last time I looked. On lunch break I was so hungry I almost ate, but my nagging hate voice kept me from stuffing my face.

The difficulties of diagnosing BDD

No one knows how many people have BDD, but its prevalence is estimated at between 1 and 2 per cent of the population. However, Dr Mark Zimmerman, Dr Jill Mattia and Dr Katharine Phillips, all experts in BDD, found that of 316 people waiting for treatment in a hospital outpatient department, 4 per cent had probable BDD, as it is currently diagnosed. Furthermore, of 500 people waiting for treatment in a psychiatric outpatient department, they found that 12 per cent had probable BDD. Unfortunately, not one diagnosis of BDD was made by their medical professional.

People with BDD tend to keep their appearance problems secret, therefore only a small number are diagnosed. Generally, it is the worry of appearing shallow that prevents them from telling the doctor how they feel about their appearance. Also, they worry that once the perceived defect is brought out into the open, others will focus on it and find it hideous. People with BDD are also concerned that mentioning the defect will prompt the other person to say there's nothing wrong, that they look normal. For BDDers, this response is a sign that the other person is not taking their emotional pain seriously.

Another reason that the number of BDD patients is difficult to determine is that the condition creates social phobia in many. They are afraid not only of going out, but also of visiting the doctor. Furthermore, because the conditions that arise with BDD such as depression and anxiety are easier to talk about than problems with appearance, BDD is often misdiagnosed. It doesn't help that people with BDD often seek help from dermatologists, cosmetic surgeons and so on rather than mental health professionals. They don't realize that BDD is a psychiatric disorder that can be treated successfully with the right kind of therapy, as discussed in Chapter 7.

In addition, diagnosis is made difficult because many medical professionals are currently not aware of BDD as a psychiatric disorder. However, they are slowly becoming enlightened, for the condition is now being debated in the media on a regular basis.

The BDD 'attack'

It is not unusual for BDDers to start the day with a BDD attack, usually in front of a secluded bedroom or bathroom mirror. This will commence with negative self-talk such as 'I look so hideous' or 'I'm sure I look worse and worse every day.' Shortly, the attack will start in earnest, comprising of self-hatred, hopelessness, isolation, feelings of impending doom and often thoughts of suicide. At the same time, the person will experience sweating, lightheadedness and palpitations. The attack may last for anything from a few minutes to a few hours, and it's a terrible time for the person and the people who care for them.

Fear is one trigger of the BDD attack. For instance, flying, a dental appointment or having to speak in public can be triggers. However, attacks are more often caused by feelings of rejection and isolation – for instance, if a person's partner is going away on business, leaving her to go on a fishing holiday with a friend, or simply working late that evening. In some people, attacks may also be triggered by the sight of a beautiful woman on a magazine cover, a handsome sportsman being interviewed on TV or a slender female singer on a TV show. Some BDDers report that it is during a BDD attack that they most feel the pain of an early trauma (see below).

Who gets BDD?

To date, BDD appears to be slightly more prevalent in females than in males. Times are rapidly changing, however, and the general consensus is that before long the condition will be distributed equally between the sexes. Males are certainly very concerned about their appearance in the media-led climate of today. They are also very open to the message that you have to be a perfect male specimen to be successful and loved. For instance, in a 2005 survey of 2,000 teenage boys with an average age of 15, published in *The British Journal of Developmental Psychology*, eight out of ten stated that they were unhappy with their appearance, 62 per cent said they disliked their faces and 68 per cent said they disliked their teeth. More than half of the boys believed themselves unattractive to girls, with 80 per cent thinking that 'getting into shape' would improve the quality of their lives and make them happier.

When boys see men like Gavin Henson, the very masculine rugby player, paying obvious attention to their appearance, male taboos of using moisturizer and tanning products are broken down. *Sneak* magazine, who carried out the survey on behalf of the above-mentioned journal, found that boys spend an average of £24 a month on grooming products, one in four boys would consider cosmetic surgery and 72 per cent would like a make-over. These results are no doubt due to the many TV cosmetic surgery and make-over shows where as many males as females are now featured.

When does BDD begin?

Studies show that BDD tends to occur in adolescence, at a time when the person is more sensitive about their appearance. However, there are numerous reports that suggest the condition can begin much earlier. Those who seek help wait for several years before finally doing so.

Do you have BDD?

To determine whether you may be suffering from BDD, answer the following questions:

• Are you excessively preoccupied with the appearance of one or more parts of your face or body that you consider unattractive or even ugly?

- Do you hate your appearance despite the fact that other people say you look fine?
- Do you constantly seek reassurance from others about your appearance?
- Has your defect(s) caused you a lot of emotional pain and distress?
- Has it restricted your social life?
- Has it interfered with your ability to concentrate at school or at work?
- Has it prevented you from attending school or work at times?
- Has it affected the lives of your family and friends?
- Do you think about your defect(s) for more than one hour a day?

If you can answer 'yes' to any one of the above questions, it is possible that you have BDD. Answer 'yes' to most or all of the questions and you are highly likely to be suffering from the disorder. Of course, for a diagnosis to be made, a psychologist would need to determine whether the defect is imagined or slight, and whether you are not really suffering from anorexia rather than BDD.

A psychologist would also need to ask a whole series of questions before he or she would be ready to give a definitive diagnosis. These might include the following:

- Do you avoid mirrors or looking in any reflective surface because you can't bear how you look?
- Do you repeatedly check yourself in mirrors and so on? If so, do you look directly at the hated body part(s) first of all?
- Do you spend a long time grooming – for example, applying make-up, shaving, combing and arranging your hair?
- Do you pick your skin in the hope of making it look better?
- Do you try to hide the hated parts of your body with a hat, long skirts, baggy clothing, make-up and so on? Do you find yourself putting up a hand to your face when someone comes close?
- Do you feel that other people will sense your defect even when it's covered?
- Do you try to hide your face by bowing your head and letting your hair swing forward?
- Do you bow your head or try to avert your face when someone is talking to you?
- If you can't hide your defect(s) do you feel uneasy and anxious?

- Do you think people are looking at you in a critical way when you're outdoors?
- Do you find it hard to go outdoors? Have there been periods when you've been housebound?
- Have you tried cosmetic surgery but don't like the result? Would you like more surgery?
- Have you had repeated cosmetic surgeries?
- Do you avoid having your photograph taken because of how you look?
- Do you search for information on BDD?
- Do you feel depressed at times because of your appearance?
- Does it make you feel angry and frustrated?
- Have you felt that life wasn't worth living because of the way you feel about your appearance?

Rituals

People with BDD are inclined to indulge in a series of rituals. These are a manifestation of obsessive-compulsive disorder and usually accompany BDD.

Grace

Grace follows the same routine every morning. After starting with a shower and getting dressed, Grace will spend a full hour brushing and arranging her hair in front of the mirror, often rewashing it because she doesn't like the effect. Her make-up ritual will then take a further hour before she is vaguely satisfied. Before finally leaving the house, she asks her partner repeatedly whether she looks all right.

She is usually late for her office job, where she spends far too much time checking herself in the bathroom mirror, reapplying more make-up and redoing her hair. In the past she has lost jobs after spending too much time in the bathroom, and she expects the same will happen with this one. At night, when her partner is in bed, she sits up into the early hours picking at her skin in the mirror. She had one or two teenage spots a few years back and now she picks at the tiny scars in an effort to make them go away. All she succeeds in doing is making her skin more scarred and then feeling she needs to shovel on the foundation to cover it.

Most people with BDD have rituals, and skin-picking is very common. It can start after a comment to the effect that the individual's complexion isn't too good, or it can occur in an effort to cover up a scar or a blemish. Those who skin-pick do it to encourage new and healthier skin growth, but generally succeed only in making scabs and more scars.

Together with skin-picking, the most common rituals are probably mirror-checking, excessive grooming, repeatedly measuring the 'faulty' body part, and touching the supposed defect. People with BDD also camouflage their 'defects' by wearing baggy clothes or a hat, constantly asking for reassurance about their appearance, making comparisons with other people and seeking repeated cosmetic surgeries.

What is the cause of BDD?

The cause of BDD is a puzzle that is yet to be solved. Many theories have been put forward, but as yet there is no conclusive evidence to back any of them up. All I can do here is repeat the theories.

Preliminary research suggests that there may be a chemical imbalance in the brains of people with BDD. There also appears to be a psychological connection, for many BDDers report a troubled upbringing or childhood trauma. Furthermore, a common denominator seems to be that most never learned to talk about their problems in childhood. Some say they always felt different from others, maybe after being tormented by a sibling, or being made an outcast by the other children in the neighbourhood. Other BDDers have, as a child, experienced physical, emotional or sexual abuse, an accident, the death of a loved one, or have endured what could have been a terminal illness.

A neurological link

A biological explanation for the development of BDD has gained ground in recent years, research suggesting there is an abnormality in the way the chemical serotonin communicates with other cells. Serotonin is an important chemical neurotransmitter that carries messages from one nerve cell to another, making them communicate with each other to function. Among other things, serotonin communication helps to dictate mood, sleep, appetite, sexual behaviour, pain and cognition (awareness, thinking and perception). It is therefore important that this neurotransmitter is working efficiently. When it is not, problems such as depression, insomnia, eating disorders, poor sex drive, heightened pain levels and difficulties with thinking and perception can arise – BDD being very much a problem of thinking and perception.

People with BDD are prescribed anti-depressants chiefly for the way they act on serotonin – hence these drugs are also known as Selective Serotonin Re-uptake Inhibitors (SSRIs). SSRIs have a beneficial effect on BDD symptoms and are often the first port of call for doctors and therapists.

Experts also believe that a shortfall of the chemical dopamine is present in BDD. Dopamine is involved in disorders of thinking and movement, and a lack of it appears to be one cause of delusional thinking. When added to SSRIs, dopamine has been shown in studies to improve obsessive-compulsive disorder, which is common in BDD.

Psychological factors

There have been psychological explanations for BDD for over a hundred years, experts suspecting that some individuals displace childhood emotional or sexual trauma onto problems with their appearance. Recent studies support this theory, for they indicate that BDD can arise as a response to sexual abuse or other trauma in childhood.

In the aftermath of some types of childhood trauma, guilt and shame can prevent a child from speaking of it to his or her family. If a person within the family itself was the cause of the trauma, it is even less likely that the problem is discussed. As a result of feeling unable to speak openly, the child can later feel she is boiling over with anger, frustration and maybe even shame if sexual abuse was the trauma. In order to cope with these feelings, she unconsciously creates BDD as a coping mechanism, displacing her agony into problems with her body. This helps her to forget about the original trauma. However, it is during a BDD attack (see above) that she is nearest to the painful feelings she experienced during the original trauma, although she may not be aware of where the painful feelings originate.

Childhood trauma can come in many different forms. They include an accident, survival of a life-threatening illness, rejection, bullying and chronic teasing. It has been found that children who are regularly teased about their looks are likely to grow up with body image disturbances. Some grow up feeling dissatisfied with their bodies but are able to live productive lives, while others develop BDD.

It is thought that painful feelings are only transferred onto a body part in people with an imbalance of the chemicals serotonin and dopamine in their brains.

Being different from other children

Children who were born with a minor 'deformity' such as protruding ears or an underbite and short lower jaw often have the problem resolved by medical intervention. However, the person's inner view of herself can fail to change and the locality of the deformity can become the focus of BDD symptoms. In the same way, if the person was overweight, had a scar, wore glasses, was fitted with dental braces, or had any feature that made her stand out as a child, she may have been seen as 'faulty' by society. Later, after losing weight, her scar healed, using contact lenses or having her teeth fixed, she can find herself unable to adapt to her improved appearance. This may explain why people who undergo several cosmetic surgeries are never happy with the result.

Personality traits

There is no evidence to suggest that BDD is a personality disorder. However, it seems that individuals of certain personality types are more predisposed to developing the condition than others. Many BDDers consider themselves to have low self-esteem and be shy, self-conscious and hypersensitive to criticism and rejection. Studies suggest that many are introverted social phobics who suffer from anxiety, depression, anger and feelings of vulnerability. There is evidence to indicate that shyness and social phobia exist before BDD develops.

A genetic link

BDD has much in common with obsessive-compulsive disorder, which is a genetic condition – it is likely to run in families. Indeed, it is in an obsessive-compulsive manner that people with BDD pursue either beauty, a normal appearance or a body image that is satisfying to themselves and society.

Media influence

BDD was a recorded disorder long before the media took its hold on the public, but there are far more cases now than ever before. Furthermore, the media preoccupation with attractiveness undoubtedly aggravates existing cases of BDD. BDDers will say that seeing a beautiful woman advertising skin cream on the TV can trigger a BDD attack (see above), as can the sight of a supermodel on a magazine cover or a handsome footballer making an appearance in town.

The two groups of people with BDD who appear to be most influenced by media images of physical attractiveness are those who compulsively compare themselves with others and those who are timid and socially phobic. In fact, a link was recently established between the latter group and media images of the 'perfect' male or female specimens.

See Chapter 1 for more information on media influence.

What is it like to suffer from BDD?

People with BDD are all different in their BDD behaviours.

Anna

Anna (27) spends hours grooming herself in the morning, taking pains to curl her hair, cutting off little bits, adding more hairspray until finally she tells herself she can't get it any better. Her make-up routine comes next. She uses a lot of foundation and takes a long time over eyeliner and lipstick, starting over again if she doesn't like the result. Anna rarely ventures outdoors, however. When she absolutely needs to buy food and other essentials, she has to force herself to go out. She finds letting people see her terrifying and always feels like she's walking oddly because of her preoccupation with how bad she looks. If someone is walking towards her, she crosses the road so they can't see her too closely. She feels like people are laughing at her everywhere she goes, and she can't bear it.

Josh

Josh (20) is in his first term at university and feels his BDD has worsened due to all the alcohol he's drinking. At one party there was a redhead he badly wanted to talk to, but he didn't because he couldn't bear for her to look at him. When his best friend left with a girl, Josh, feeling desperate, dashed out of the party and cried on his bed for two hours while tormenting himself with his defects. He feels that his self-hatred has ruined his life and that he'll never have a girlfriend. All he wants is to be normal, but is afraid that will never happen.

Callum

Callum (17) can't get away from the feeling that a black cloud is hanging over him. He's aware that people are constantly trying to get close to him, but he keeps on pushing them away – even the ones who attempt to understand his BDD. When a girl in his sixth form class offered to help him, he swore at her and marched away. Now she has no time for him and he regrets his behaviour deeply.

Jenny

In the last few years, Jenny (37) has spent over £20,000 on cosmetic surgery and she's already thinking about this year's nip 'n' tuck. She's had a facelift, eyelift, chin and neck lift, facial liposuction, fat grafting into her cheeks, rhinoplasty, lip augmentation, breast implants and extensive liposuction. However, it's not made a scrap of difference in how she feels about her appearance. She constantly compares herself with other women and finds herself lacking.

Rosemary

Rosemary (49) repeatedly asks her husband for reassurance about her appearance. He always tells her she looks fine, but on her down days she suspects he's only saying that to make her feel better. She's had BDD for 33 years and still can't venture out without wearing long skirts to hide her 'thick' legs, long sleeves to conceal her 'bat wing' arms and polo neck jumpers to cover her 'turkey' neck. A few weeks ago Rosemary plucked up the courage to go on her once yearly trip for new clothes. Her husband encouraged her to try on a couple of three-quarter sleeved tops with round necks, but once in the changing room she felt panicky and couldn't tear herself away from the mirror. She'd never minded her cheekbones, but now she saw them as much flatter and was terrified. For a whole hour she kept touching them in the hope they would change back to how they were before. Her husband eventually asked the assistant to lead her out. She hadn't tried on the clothes.

Other conditions that can exist with BDD

As with eating disorders, BDD is generally accompanied by an array of other disorders.

Depression

Of people with depression, it is estimated that 8 per cent also suffer from BDD. This is not really surprising, for the majority of people with BDD experience depression at some point in their illness. The depression can be severe, the person unable to eat, sleep or even get out of bed. Suicide may be seen as the only solution. Fortunately, Selective Serotonin Re-uptake Inhibitors (SSRIs) can not only beat the depression, they can also reduce the symptoms of BDD.

Anxiety

The anxiety associated with BDD can include worry and fear, or it can take a more physical form such as headaches, extreme tiredness and stomach upsets. Many people with BDD experience panic attacks in which they sweat, have difficulty breathing, experience heart palpitations and have feelings of intense anxiety. An attack is often triggered by an image of 'perfection' in the media. (See Chapter 7 for advice on controlling anxiety.)

Obsessive-compulsive disorder

The ritualistic behaviour that comes with BDD is caused by obsessive-compulsive disorder (OCD for short). OCD is an anxiety disorder in which the individual will either suffer the persistent intrusion of unwanted thoughts into his or her awareness, or an overwhelming compulsion to carry out a specific behavioural or cognitive (of the mind) ritual. However hard they try to stop the intrusive thoughts or ritualistic behaviour, they find themselves unable to. In fact, they experience severe anxiety until the ritual is finished. People with OCD tend to fear an imagined consequence if the ritual is not performed exactly as their OCD dictates.

SSRI medication can effectively decrease the symptoms of OCD.

Social phobia

Also called Social Anxiety Disorder, social phobia is the most common of all the anxiety disorders. It is characterized by a marked and persistent fear of social situations in which embarrassment may occur. In people with BDD, social phobia arises because they expect their appearance to cause them embarrassment. Unfortunately some BDDers are diagnosed only with social phobia, for they are too embarrassed to mention the way they feel about their bodies.

Your doctor

If you think you have BDD, it is strongly advised that you see your doctor, for a great deal can be done to reduce the symptoms. Your doctor is likely to start by prescribing SSRIs. However, you would be best to also accept a referral to a local psychiatric unit where psychotherapy, counselling and cognitive behavioural therapy can be given, to great effect. SSRIs can be taken in conjunction with such therapy.

Medications

SSRI medications are particularly effective for people with BDD. Generally used for their anti-depressant qualities, SSRIs counteract the obsessive thinking and compulsive behaviour that are present in BDD. These drugs can also alleviate the depression, anxiety, panic and social phobia that usually accompany the disorder.

People who respond well to SSRIs are able to more easily push aside obsessive thoughts and get on with their lives. Moreover, the 'defects' in some people seem far less noticeable in their minds and they are more able to cope with any negative thoughts about their appearance. Compulsive behaviours are no longer compulsive, as a result of which BDDers can find themselves able to refrain from skin-picking, mirror-checking and so on. With the reduction of anxiety and depression comes a boost in self-confidence, and patients are likely to start wearing less camouflaging clothes and bothering less with make-up and their hair. All in all, SSRIs are an enormous help to most individuals with BDD. They can even be of benefit to those who are suicidal.

It is important that you keep your doctor informed of your progress. He or she has the option of prescribing different SSRIs if the first one you are prescribed fails to have the desired effect.

Cognitive behavioural therapy (CBT)

Evidence suggests that medication and cognitive behavioural techniques can complement each other well. Under the guidance of a skilled therapist, the behavioural aspect of BDD is carefully addressed, the therapist perhaps focusing first on exposure. This involves gradually confronting the situations the individual had most feared, such as going into public places, attending parties, talking to someone face to face and so on without hiding or camouflaging the embarrassing area. With repeated exposure, the anxiety and fear should gradually decrease. However, prior to physically confronting a person's fears, exposure can be carried out mentally by the individual repeatedly imagining themselves in the feared situation. This type of exposure works surprisingly well.

Response prevention will also be tackled. This involves encouraging the person to refuse to carry out compulsive behaviours such as skin-picking, mirror-checking, measuring, comparing with others and asking for reassurance. Patients will learn that when they are able to delay such behaviours for long enough, the impulse to do them is more likely to abate. Patients are also given a set time, such as 15 minutes, to groom themselves in a morning and before going out in the evening. As people with BDD are typically never satisfied with how they look, giving them a set time for grooming can cause them less anxiety than allowing them to stop when they finally realize they can do no better.

CBT also includes family education, group therapy and counselling. These are designed to help family members understand the exact nature of the problem, what may be going wrong with family life and how to help and support the person with BDD.

For advice on how to stop negative thinking and automatic thoughts, how to improve your body image, information on anxiety control and for a relaxation exercise, turn to Chapter 7. However, you are strongly advised to also seek medical and psychiatric help for your condition. If such treatments have failed in the past, it is always possible to ask for different medication (see above) or a repeat referral to a psychiatric unit. Being motivated to succeed is the first and perhaps most important requirement for a favourable outcome, so try to give it your all this time.

6

Alcoholism

Alcohol is like food in that it can be used to push away emotional pain that often has its roots in low self-esteem – common components of poor body image. It's also commonly found together with poor eating habits. Hence its discussion in this book.

An addiction to alcohol is a massive problem in modern society, with one in four adults regularly drinking quantities that can be dangerous to health. It can begin early, for recent studies suggest that four out of ten 15 year olds drink alcohol in any one week. Of girls aged between 10 and 15 years, wine is the favoured tipple, and of boys the same age, beer and lager are preferred. Research has shown that 24 per cent of 12 year olds and 44 per cent of 13 year olds have consumed at least one of these drinks.

Young people and alcohol

Young adults tend to binge-drink, their total consumption often occurring on Friday and Saturday nights. There is evidence to suggest that some 13 to 16 year olds consume at least five alcoholic drinks in one session, perhaps the start of a binge-drinking habit. Most alcohol is purchased from off-licences, with the pub as the next source and then the supermarket. Research also shows that alcohol bought by young people is more likely to be connected to alcohol abuse and public nuisance than alcohol for use in the home. In the UK, over 1,000 youngsters under 15 are taken to hospital each year with alcohol poisoning.

Alcopops

Since their introduction into the UK in 1995, pre-mixed spirits called 'alcopops' have become increasingly popular for youngsters because of their high alcoholic content and fruit flavour that disguises the taste of alcohol. Their 5 per cent alcohol content is greater than that of normal strength beers, and some alcopops are 'buzz' drinks that contain large amounts of stimulants such as caffeine.

The fastest growing drink of all time, they feed into an already increased drinking pattern for youngsters – 10 per cent of underaged drinkers drink them on a regular basis.

The problems caused by alcohol abuse

Alcohol is absorbed into the bloodstream and has an effect on the person within one to five minutes. The effect can last for several hours depending on other factors such as how much alcohol was drunk, whether there was food in the stomach, the person's body weight, and how used to drinking the person is, or their tolerance to alcohol.

After drinking about four units of alcohol (two pints of beer or lager), the person feels less inhibited and much more relaxed. However, alcohol is a depressant. It slows down the nervous system, the reactions, and the way the body functions. Moreover, the mind is less able to reason. The person may now become aggressive, throwing insults around or picking a fight.

The severity of a hangover is dependent on substances called cogeners that add flavour and colour to drinks. As a rule, the darker the drink the more cogeners it contains. Gin and vodka are the kindest spirits, whereas brandy, whisky and cognac can cause the worst hangovers. Of wines, red wine contains a chemical called tyramine that can produce a severe headache in some people. White wine is far more gentle.

Alcohol has a greater effect on women than men because we tend to weigh less, we have lower concentrations of a particular enzyme that breaks down alcohol in our stomachs, and we have 10 per cent less fluid in our bodies than men. Because alcohol has a diuretic effect, body fluids are reduced further, often causing dehydration and a hangover, to which women are also more prone.

Excess alcohol literally poisons the brain, irritates the intestines and leads to dehydration – causing severe headache, irritability, jumpiness, shakiness, vertigo, nausea, vomiting, indigestion and diarrhoea. Long-term heavy drinking can cause inflammation of the stomach (gastritis), liver (hepatitis) and pancreas (pancreatitis). It can also give rise to brain damage, memory loss, mood swings, personality changes and obesity – the latter arising because alcohol is high in calories. It can increase the risk of cancer, as well. Too much alcohol at one time can slow down the body to the point where it stops working altogether. A fatal unplanned overdose of heroin or tranquillizers can occur when the person has been drinking, for alcohol and drugs are a dangerous and unpredictable combination.

How much alcohol is bad for you?

One or two units of alcohol a day is beneficial for some people. It reduces stress levels, and the antioxidants in drinks such as red wine can limit the risk of a heart attack. Recent research suggests, however, that drinking just one unit of alcohol a day can increase the risk of breast cancer in women.

How much alcohol is safe?

The maximum safe daily alcohol intake for women is no more than two to three units, with some alcohol-free days in between. For men it is three to four units with some alcohol-free days in between. The weekly safe limit for women is no more than 14 units, and for men it is a maximum of 21 units.

So what is a unit?

- Half a pint of normal strength beer, lager or cider equals one unit.
- One small (100 ml) glass of wine equals one unit.
- A large (175 ml) glass of wine equals two units.
- A single (25 ml) measure of spirits equals one unit.
- One 275 ml bottle of alcopop (5.5 per cent/volume) equals 1.5 units.

It is generally accepted that for a woman to drink more than 35 units of alcohol a week is dangerous to her health. For a man, the dangerous level is 50 units.

The dangers of drinking

Alcohol intoxication is very common. In fact, nearly half the male population and one in seven women will have been drunk in the past three months. The following can occur when a person is intoxicated:

- Drink-driving related accidents.
- Falls and accidents.
- Undesirable sexual situations or less practice of safe sex.
- Loss of consciousness and subsequently choking on their own vomit.
- Pregnant women who drink six or more units of alcohol a day (see below) may give birth to babies with alcohol withdrawal symptoms, hare lip or other facial abnormalities, coupled with retardation of physical and mental development. Abnormalities

due to the mother drinking too much are called Foetal Alcohol
Syndrome. Lesser degrees of drinking can cause the baby to have
a low birth weight.

- People who drink to excess generally make the people around
  them unhappy. Often, family life is strained by the financial
  difficulties the drinking causes. It can even break down altogether.
  It is possible that violence and other forms of crime associated
  with loss of control may occur within the family home.
- Alcohol-related deaths, which have increased almost every year
  since 1979.

Are you addicted to alcohol?

Alcohol is a socially acceptable drug, often part of celebrations,
casual get-togethers and daily working life, and a person can be
surprised at how much they actually consume. However, it is when
you start to crave alcohol that you know you are addicted.

A practical definition of dependent drinking or alcoholism is
persistent drinking that interferes with the person's health, legal
position, interpersonal relationships or means of livelihood. In the
UK, there are four million heavy drinkers, 800,000 problem drinkers
and 400,000 dependent drinkers, or alcoholics.

Your answers to these questions may help you to decide whether
or not you are addicted:

- Do you regularly drink more than you intended?
- Do you crave drink for much of the time?
- Do you drink to escape worries or troubles?
- Do you feel guilty about your drinking?
- Is your drinking causing a problem in any area of your life – for
  example, relationships, work, finances, legal or health?
- Does anyone frequently complain about your drinking?

If you have answered 'yes' to two or more of these questions, I'm
afraid you have a serious problem. To check on your health
situation, it is advisable that you request a medical examination.
People in the early stages of alcohol addiction are likely to not yet
have developed serious problems.

Starting to accept that alcohol is a problem in your life has to be
your first important step towards recovery. If you have tried and

failed to overcome your addiction in the past, give yourself another chance. You don't have to tackle the problem alone – there are several responsible organizations set up to help people to defeat their alcoholism.

Alcohol withdrawal

Alcohol withdrawal is difficult for the truly addicted and, unfortunately, few are able to give up without medical intervention in a detoxification unit. Most successful programmes are either part of the Alcoholics Anonymous network (see below) or employ their techniques.

The symptoms of alcohol withdrawal usually occur within 12 to 72 hours after the last drink of alcohol. Major withdrawal symptoms may occur for up to 7 days, with recurring symptoms lasting for several months, and may include anxiety, depression, excessive sweating – especially on the hands and face, fatigue, hallucinations, headache, insomnia, irritability, nausea and vomiting, nervousness, palpitations, rapid heartbeat, shaking and tremors, trouble concentrating and seizures.

If left untreated, alcohol withdrawal can lead to a more serious set of symptoms called delirium tremens ('the DTs') which can appear 2 to 10 days after the drinking stops. The DTs start with rising anxiety, then become confusion, severe depression, difficulty sleeping, nightmares, disorientation, hallucinations, excessive sweating, fever, and illusions that arouse restlessness and fears.

Organizations that can help

The most influential organization in history to help alcoholics recover is Alcoholics Anonymous (AA). There are AA branches all over the world and currently over a million members. Meetings are positive and hopeful, giving acceptance and support to people who are experiencing very difficult times. Members also feel they have the support of their fellow recovering alcoholics in the room. (See Useful Addresses.)

Alcohol Concern is a national voluntary agency that acts as an umbrella body for 500 local agencies that give information and advice about alcohol-related problems. The agency works to promote awareness of alcohol issues and can tell the individual and their families where to find the most appropriate help. Alcohol Concern does not operate a helpline or provide actual services to people with alcohol problems. However, there are drop-in centres for information and advice. (Again, see Useful Addresses.)

Treatment

Once you have made a commitment to overcome your drinking problem, your local GP should be your first port of call. As well as taking blood tests to check your state of health, GPs can make referrals to a number of units depending on your situation and local availability.

Treatment in a detoxification unit is likely to begin with an injection of vitamin B1, particularly if you are suffering from malnutrition due to a poor diet. While you are undergoing withdrawal symptoms, you can be assured of receiving plenty of rest, good nutrition and emotional support. For people who suffer severe withdrawal symptoms, a nervous system depressant such as benzodiazepine is prescribed with a dosage that is tapered down over 3 to 5 days. In addition, each patient is given a full medical assessment followed by the appropriate intervention.

Diet, including supplements and fluid, is an important factor, for alcoholics seldom eat properly. In one trial, recovering alcoholics on a normal hospital diet were compared with those on a special diet which excluded caffeinated coffee, junk food, dairy products and peanut butter. After six months, less than 38 per cent of those on the hospital diet had remained sober, compared with over 81 per cent on the special diet (R. M. Guenther, 1983). In another trial where sugar was restricted, complex carbohydrates increased and caffeine cut out, there was a marked reduction in alcohol craving (J. R. Biery, 1991).

7

Recovery

The earlier an eating disorder, Body Dysmorphic Disorder (BDD) or alcoholism is recognized for what it is, the quicker and less painful are treatment and recovery. Delay in recognition can cause the disorder to become more severe and deep-seated, and recovery to be difficult and protracted. The hardest part is accepting the problem and acknowledging that you need help. If you have an eating disorder, it may have been a part of your life for many years but you never seriously got round to doing anything about it. Anorexics can be particularly opposed to accepting that anything is wrong, thus the average time between onset of anorexia and treatment is five years. However, forcing a person to have treatment rarely works. For success, co-operation is required.

Whether you have an eating disorder, BDD or alcoholism, the fact that you are reading this book shows that you would like things to change. However, moving from this point to full recovery will be the most difficult thing you have done in your life – some of you may not achieve that completely – but it will be the best thing you have ever done, whether occasional relapses occur or not.

In order to motivate yourself further, remind yourself of how alone you feel, and how unhappy. If you have experienced shame and self-disgust over your behaviour you may have avoided romantic relationships, but you know deep down that to have a partner in life would be wonderful. It would be someone with whom to share the good times and bad, someone to go places with, or just to snuggle up to on the sofa at night. Alternately, you may wish to renew old friendships and make some new ones, or apply for a new job, go to university, on a course, or take up a new hobby. Many of these things are difficult when you are obsessed with food, drink or your looks. For one thing, it is not always easy to concentrate on anything but your particular obsession and the problems in your life. However, with treatment and self-help, you can start to get on with your life and really enjoy it.

Whether you think your disorder is serious or not, or whether you don't believe your physical and emotional well-being are impaired or at risk, you will feel a million times better if you can learn to eat and drink normally and improve your body image and self-esteem.

Before you begin your new venture, try to follow these important steps:

- Start by making a realistic mental picture of where you would like to end up when you are free of your problem. For instance, would you like to be a trained nurse, working hard on the wards and having a fun social life? Or maybe you would like to complete a graphic art course, get married, have children and work part-time as a web designer from home? What was the career path you always wanted to follow until your problem got in the way? Now visualize how to get on to that path and see yourself doing so in the near future.
- Now visualize how you would like yourself to be. For instance, you may want to be successful, friendly and happy. If so, try as hard as you can to see yourself that way. Empty your mind of troubles and cares and start to imagine the shining feeling you would have about your whole persona if you were successful, respected and thoroughly enjoyed your job. Now imagine how light your heart would feel if you were very friendly towards other people. Last, imagine the sense of freedom you would feel from being a happy person with no worries at all.
- Next you should make a real commitment to change. This may seem alarming, but you are not about to do something you have not done before. You were free from your problem once; you can be free from it again! Write down 'I will take control of my life' in bold on four or five large sheets of paper and pin them on the wall of each room in your house. Every time you look at one, let the words really sink in and know for certain that you are about to change.
- There may be no time that seems 'right' to start to change, so make a commitment to start tomorrow morning, as soon as you get up. And stick to it, no matter what!
- Keeping a diary will be enormously helpful, for you will be able to record your use of the techniques you are about to learn. Use a new notebook, buying one today if you don't have one. By the time the notebook is full, you will be a long way down the road to recovery.

Before we go on, I would like you to congratulate yourself for having the courage to start to take control of your life and to fight for changes. It takes some doing. Every time you feel afraid and consider returning to the familiar pattern, remind yourself that your problem is no longer in control of you – you yourself are now the boss.

I suggest that you read through each section of advice before following the instructions. You may need to refer to this book again and again, so keep it close. If something goes wrong, don't feel you have failed and give up on the whole process. You will have failures, for your problem won't be too willing to give up the ferocity of its grip. Keep at it and let each small success feel good.

If you have real difficulty following the instructions, you will be best advised to see a skilled therapist who can lead you sensitively through each process.

Who may not benefit

The self-help instructions in this book are likely not to be appropriate for those in the following categories:

- Those who are fixed into a rigid pattern of grossly disturbed eating habits/BDD behaviours or alcohol consumption. If you are willing to try to change, you are not in this category.
- Those who are isolated completely. To gain dominance over their problem, people who live isolated lives are likely to need the support of a therapist they can see regularly.
- Those with a very low body weight. People with severe malnutrition (usually those with anorexia) should first and foremost seek help from a therapist.
- Those who are so depressed they can't summon the motivation to try to change. Such people should visit their doctor for a possible prescription of anti-depressant medication. These drugs can make a terrific difference. It may then be possible for you to follow this programme.
- Those for whom their eating disorder/BDD or alcoholism is only a part of a larger problem. This includes people who self-harm and people with serious relationship problems.
- Those with an eating disorder and a medical condition related to eating, such as diabetes. Medical help should be sought in this case.
- Those who are pregnant. Again, medical help should be sought first of all.

If you belong to one of the above categories, you should ask your doctor for a referral for specialist treatment. The prospects of recovery are good with such treatment. For everyone else, try to see the programme in this chapter as a starting point, something you can move on from to specialist treatment, if need be. The latter is always an option, whether you have had such treatment in the past or not.

Making a start

The first stage in your recovery programme is to establish exactly where you are now. Take an honest look at your life, then read the following points and write down your thoughts at the back of your notebook. Be completely honest with yourself, for facing up to the reality of your current situation is an essential part of the recovery process.

- If you have an eating disorder, try to remember what prompted you to go on your first diet. Did you tell yourself you would be more popular if you were slim, and that everybody diets? If you are anorexic, was it a sense of achievement at your weight loss that made you want to continue to diet? Did you feel strong and in control for being able to diet so successfully?
- If you are a compulsive overeater, ask yourself if there is a hidden gain to being overweight? Does extra weight provide a feeling of protection? Is it a kind of armour? Is it a means of hiding from your sexuality or sexual identity? Is eating a way of controlling your mood? Do you use food and eating to cover up unconscious beliefs and past traumas? Do you use food and your body to tell a story for which you have no language?
- If you have an eating disorder, try to pinpoint the things that may be maintaining it. If you binge, what is it that compels you to do so? How exactly do you feel before you binge? How do you feel during? How do you feel after? If you purge, try to pinpoint exactly how that makes you feel. Be completely honest.
- If you have BDD, try to remember what triggered your first concerns about your appearance. Did you experience some kind of trauma? Did you feel unable to speak of this trauma to your family? Were you teased about your appearance at school? Was there something that made you feel different from other children or adolescents, such as glasses, dental braces, a scar or acne? Did

you once have an abnormality, such as scoliosis of the spine, a squint, a short lower jaw and underbite? Have these conditions been resolved by medical intervention, yet your mind still tells you there's a problem?

- If you have BDD, how exactly do you feel when you know someone is looking at your 'defect'? How do you feel when grooming? How do you feel before venturing outdoors? If you hide away, what exactly are you frightened may happen?
- If you are an alcoholic, try to recall if something specific happened that turned you from a normal drinker to drinking to excess. Did you start drinking a lot because your friends drank a lot? Do you drink to feel better? Do you drink to forget something painful? If so, what exactly is it that hurts so much? How do you feel while you are drinking? How does drinking affect your life?

Your particular problem is likely to have developed as a means of dealing with something unpleasant in your life. To help to organize your thoughts, do the following – perhaps with the help of a trusted friend:

- Make a list of the advantages gained by your problem.
- After you've done that, make a list of the disadvantages.

Don't be surprised if, at this stage, the advantages outweigh the disadvantages, if you're being entirely honest. Your problem may have been a good friend – but it was a friend who wouldn't give you any peace, who did a lot of damage to your life.

Look a few years ahead

Now imagine seeing a friend and explaining to her what your life is like now, what you've been doing and where you've been. Imagine seeing that same friend after a five-year interval and giving her a rundown of what you've been up to and where you've been in the meantime. It's often when you can look a few years ahead and see how much life you have missed out on due to your particular problem that you realize how it is holding you back. You are likely to see, also, that your determination to change is exactly the right thing.

Imagine seeing that friend after a ten-year interval and only being able to say, 'My life is still dominated by food/my appearance/drink. I dropped out of college and never went into the career I used to talk about. I don't really go anywhere and I haven't made any new friends. I'm too much of a mess to enter into any type of romantic relationship, and life's a battle all the time.'

In comparison, your friend may be doing well in her chosen career, she may have got married and have travelled with her husband to Australia the previous spring; she may have made some new friends and be joining them in a weekly 'kick boxing' class, and she may be looking forward to getting pregnant in the next year or so. Well, you can be that person too!

Challenging negative thinking

We don't normally question our own thinking – we're often not even aware of the thoughts running around in our heads. However, when our thoughts are very negative we tend to believe they are accurate and true, and that can fuel problematic behaviour. For instance, a man who thinks he's no good with money will stop trying to be good with money; a girl who is sure she'll fail her exams will not bother to revise and then fail her exams. These negative thoughts are irrational untruths that determine our behaviour and even the paths our lives take.

The following automatic thoughts and beliefs are examples of the internal world of a person with an eating disorder or BDD:

- I hate my body. If I lost some weight, people would like me more.
- My life would be far better if I was slim/better looking.
- Being so fat/ugly makes me feel useless.
- I'll never look like I want to look.

An alcoholic might think:

- No one will ever take a loser like me seriously.
- I'm too unreliable to ever have settled down. That's one reason my relationship is falling apart.
- I'll be getting the sack soon because I'm so careless.

Luckily, such irrational thoughts and beliefs can be turned around. You can learn a new, more positive approach to life. First, you need to acknowledge your irrational thoughts and beliefs for what they are, and for the behaviour they induce. Upcoming family celebrations commonly provoke great anxiety in people with an eating disorder, BDD or alcoholism. Actually writing down your negative thoughts and feelings at the back of your notebook, and really analysing them, can make the fact that they are irrational crystal clear to you. It makes you more aware.

Example 1 shows possible irrational thoughts and feelings prior to a family party:

Example 1.

Situation	Irrational thoughts	Irrational feelings
Family Party	They'll all think I'm hideous because I'm so fat/ugly. No one will want to talk to me. I'll spoil the whole event.	I will then feel sad and alienated. I will hate myself for the way I look and for being such a misery.

This example illustrates just how irrational an eating disorder or BDD can make a person. Yet without analysis, the potential repercussions can be staggering. In this situation, you may end up talking yourself into staying at home, experiencing mixed self-pity, guilt and self-loathing. Your decision could even cause an argument with the person whose party it is.

The alcoholic would dread the party for fear of getting very drunk and making a fool of him or herself. If the alcohol addiction had been kept secret from the family, the person would also be afraid of being found out and being viewed as the failure they see themselves as. They might even fear being rejected by their family, which would be too much to bear. These are irrational thoughts that may make them avoid the party, hurting the people they love most.

Whatever your particular problem, try to imagine what your own thoughts and feelings would be prior to a family party, then look objectively at what you have written. Are your thoughts and feelings reasonable? Do you ever know for certain what other people are thinking? Surely you would feel like you were spoiling the occasion if you sat with a face as long as a fiddle and made no effort to talk to anyone. And are your relatives really so anti-social they would disregard you? Would they choose to reject you rather than help if they knew you had a problem with drink?

When we challenge negative feelings thus, the reality of the situation soon becomes apparent. People make an effort to be friendly at family gatherings. Your fellow guests are people you know well. Common ground can always be found, should you wish to look for it. If you have a drink problem, most relatives would prefer to know about it than not. They might shout at you at first, but it's odds on that they'll want to help.

So, you have re-evaluated and subsequently vanquished one set of negative thoughts – only to find it swiftly replaced by another. You have decided to attend the party, but now, if you have an eating disorder, you are worrying about eating in company. Will the desire to eat totally consume you? Will you start bingeing in front of everyone? Will they be alarmed and think you are disgusting?

Writing down your thoughts helps you to look at them in a more detached light, as you can see from Example 2. In this example, I have incorporated a column listing possible solutions.

Example 2

Situation	Irrational thoughts	Irrational feelings	Solution
Seeing lots of food at the party	The vision of all that food will make me want to binge. I won't be able to stop myself.	I will binge and everyone will be horrified. They will think I'm a greedy fat pig.	Sit so you can't see the food before the buffet starts. Copy the next person re the amount of food you put on your plate. Sit so you can't see the table again.

Here, irrational feelings are seen for what they are, and possible solutions are considered. If you have BDD, imagine attending the family party and hating the fact that people are looking at you, imagine they will think you so ugly they are only grateful they don't look like you. Imagine your personal irrational thoughts and feelings and write them down. Now turn your mind to coming up with a solution. This may involve observing that the other guests are far from perfect themselves, counting to ten if your heart starts racing, then perhaps speaking to someone you know well. When you next come across a dilemma and start thinking irrationally, write down your thoughts. Now consider the possible solutions.

The same system exactly applies to alcoholics. When you meet a problem, instead of reaching for the bottle, write down your thoughts and feelings, look at them detachedly and see them for what they really are. If they truly are irrational, try to think of a solution. Whether you are able to act on that solution is another matter, but the more you set your mind to thinking of solutions, the easier it will be to act on them.

Keep the notebook at your side and try to get into the habit of writing down all your negative thoughts as they pass through your mind. See each one from different perspectives and decide honestly whether it is irrational. If it is, think of the irrational feelings such a thought might provoke, and of course the resulting behaviour. Knowing negative thoughts for what they are is another great leap along that road to recovery.

Problem-solving

Someone with an eating disorder is likely to binge-eat in response to a problem, an alcoholic will drink in response to a problem and a person with BDD will see a particular part of themselves as more unattractive than ever. Often the problem is obvious, but at other times it may not be so easy to ascertain what exactly is bothering you. You may know only that you feel anxious and unhappy and are more susceptible to the impulse to binge, drink or feel unsightly. It is therefore essential that you try to identify the problem.

You can learn to deal with problems by following these steps:

- Think hard about what the problem actually is, then write it down as clearly as possible on a page at the back of your notebook.
- Contemplate all the possible solutions to your problem, wild as some of them may seem. Write them all down.
- Look hard at all the solutions, thinking of what exactly is involved. Decide which of your solutions you could realistically go ahead with, and whether it would be effective.
- Act on the solution you have chosen.
- After the event, look at what has happened and consider whether your solution was effective. If things didn't work out, reflect on what you might have done to produce a better outcome.

This problem-solving technique is widely used and with great success. In time, working out solutions will become second nature.

You should even be able to break destructive cycles in close relationships, helping you to feel happier and more capable.

8

Changing Your Eating Behaviour

Before changes can be made to the way you eat, it is important that you know exactly what is happening with your eating just now. You can do this by keeping a detailed daily record of when you eat, what you eat, where you eat, whether you felt it was excessive, whether you felt out of control, whether you vomited or took laxatives, and whether you used exercise to burn off the calories. Becoming aware of your eating habits may make you feel worse at first, but in order that you make essential changes in this area, it is crucial that you know exactly where you are now.

Monitoring charts

To record what you eat, use a full page of your notebook every day. Don't just write down the things you are happy about eating, and don't be afraid to record everything when you binge. The record will be excellent to look back on when you're eating normally once more. Keep the notebook with you at all times, and write down what you have eaten immediately after doing so. Trying to remember everything at the end of the day simply won't work. There will always be things you forget.

Look at the example chart below, then mark up several pages in your notebook with the date and headings.

Date: 11 May 2006

Time	Food and drink	Place	Ex/Vom/Lax	Thoughts
8 am	3 cups black coffee	Kitchen	Exercised	Feel fat. Dieting.
9.30 am	2 cups black coffee	Kitchen		ditto
12 pm	2 cups tea	Kitchen		ditto
2.30 pm	1 slim-fast milk shake, glass of water	Kitchen		ditto
4.05 pm	1 cup of black coffee	Kitchen		ditto

Time	Food	Place		Feelings
5.50 pm	Scrambled egg with 1 slice of toast, 1 cup black coffee	Kitchen		Hungry
6.25 pm	2 cheeseburgers, chips, mushy peas, thick slice of cream cake, large bar of chocolate, half a tub of ice-cream, 3 banana milk shakes	Bedroom	Vomit Exercised	Couldn't fit into that size 10 top. Very upset! Disgusted with myself!
7.15 pm	Remainder of ice cream. Another large bar chocolate. A second thick slice of cream cake. 2 glasses milk	Bedroom	Vomit	Feel I'll never be thin. My life's a total mess.
9.40 pm	Cup of black coffee	Lounge		Feel depressed.

Reviewing your monitoring charts

When you have monitored your eating for a week, look at the week as a whole and try to identify any patterns in your eating. These patterns will be particularly evident in people who binge-eat. For instance:

• Is there a time of day when you eat less?
• Is there a particular time when binges are likely to take place?
• Are there times when you can more easily control your eating?
• Are there specific situations that trigger your binges?
• Is there a particular type of food that you eat during binges?
• Are there periods of time when you eat nothing at all?
• Are these periods often followed by binges?
• Are days when you diet generally followed by binges?

When you think carefully about your answers to these questions, several things may become evident. For example, it may be clear that you are less hungry in a morning and early afternoon, so exist on not much more than black coffee. You may then feel ravenous later in the day and tend to binge. It is far better to break up your eating throughout the day, as seen below – even if you don't feel hungry in a morning. That way you are less tempted to binge, or to eat junk food in general.

Guidelines for normal eating

Normal eating is meant to be a relaxed, stress-free affair. It is meant to take a far less prominent role in your life than it currently does. Below is a list of the basic guidelines for normal healthy eating – they are not rules, so should not be rigidly adhered to. It might be best to view them as a set of goals towards which you should aim.

- Eat in company, if possible.
- Don't be distracted while eating. Avoid watching TV, reading, doing a crossword puzzle, sending a text message, talking on the phone and so on. It is advisable that you only talk to the people around you or listen to music.
- Keep to regular eating times.
- Eat proper breakfast foods at breakfast time (cereal, porridge, toast and so on); eat proper lunch foods at lunch time (sandwiches, beans on toast, baked potato with tuna and so on), and eat proper evening meal foods at evening meal time (chicken curry, a roast dinner, spaghetti bolognese and so on).
- Plan your meals beforehand so you know exactly what you'll be eating and when you'll be eating it.

Try to keep these guidelines in mind as you go through the week, but don't attempt to put them all into action. For now it is sufficient to work on one of them each week, maybe starting with breakfast, then going on to lunch, then working on your evening meal, noting everything you eat on your food monitoring chart. At the end of each week, look at your chart and note any changes in the way you are eating, whether good or bad. Consider how any good changes were made and whether you found them difficult or easy. Now congratulate yourself for taking a fantastic leap along the road to normal eating!

If, after the first week, you forgot to write down a lot of what you ate, or could not put in action any of the guidelines for normal eating, don't be discouraged. Simply go back to the beginning and start again. If this seems like a chore, remember that it's a chore with the capacity of starting to lift your life out of the doldrums.

It may be helpful at this time to take up a former interest so you are not constantly thinking of food. Of course, the interest should not be food-orientated, like cookery, baking or cake decorating. You may once have enjoyed drawing, reading, writing, sewing, knitting, making model aircraft, learning a language or playing the guitar. Taking up this interest again is likely to be relaxing, distracting and provide feelings of achievement. This is perhaps not a good time to take up a new interest, however, for you may be too delicate at the moment to cope with the challenge.

Making a meal plan

The next stage of the recovery programme is for people with an eating disorder and entails learning to eat regular meals in a way that is controlled. This means eating breakfast, lunch and evening meal, with two or three snacks in between. Eating regular meals in this way, with weight-loss diet and binges abandoned, will not make you overweight. Instead, it will help your body to find its natural weight – after all, humans were not intended to be either fat or thin, but somewhere in between. And it is the 'somewhere in between' stage that is most healthy and vital. It is also the most physically attractive stage, if you care to ask members of the opposite sex.

Forming your plan

It is important that you eat at set times rather than when you feel hungry or just feel you need food. People with an eating disorder cannot trust their sensations of hunger or fullness at this early stage and you should try your very best to ignore them. Look at the sample meal plan below and write down the most suitable times for you to have breakfast, dinner and evening meal.

Add to that the times you would prefer to have two or three snacks. There should be no more than a three or four-hour gap between eating times. These times should then be strictly adhered to – that is, you should make doubly sure that you eat at these times, even if you don't feel particularly hungry. If you postpone your meal, your appetite will increase and binge-eaters are highly likely to want to binge later on. Between the times specified for eating, you should try your very best to eat nothing at all.

Below is a sample meal plan:

8.00 am	Breakfast
10.30 am	Snack
1.00 pm	Lunch

3.30 pm	Snack
6.30 pm	Evening meal
9.30 pm	Snack

Don't be alarmed by the number of eating times in the plan. Your own plan should be similar, depending on your particular routine. If you feel hungry when you are not supposed to eat, the short period between eating times means you can hearten yourself with the knowledge that you can eat before too long.

People with anorexia may find it difficult at first to eat five or six times a day. For this reason, you should start by having one main meal – say lunch – followed by a snack. After a week of eating one meal and a snack, a second meal and a snack can be introduced. In the third week, it may be possible for you to eat three normal meals a day, accompanied by two or three snacks. If this rate of increase is too fast for you, increase the number of normal meals you have at your own pace, so long as there is a gradual increase.

Choosing your food

The food you choose to eat in your meals and snacks is not very important at this stage. However, it should be food that you are happy about eating without it leading to a binge or you wanting to purge. If you are unsure of the amounts you should be eating, watch what the people around you eat – particularly those who are viewed as 'normal' eaters. If you live a fairly isolated life, now is the time to confide in someone you trust. I'm sure that person will be only too happy to give you guidance on portion sizes and so on.

In order that you are not confused about what exactly to eat, it is essential that you plan your meals in advance. It is recommended that you jot down your plan every evening on top of the next day's food monitoring sheet.

In anorexia (and bulimia where the person is very thin), the weight gained in the early stages of recovery is made up of a higher proportion of muscle tissue and water than fat. Therefore, very little of the weight you gain is fat and you really have no need to panic or feel anxious.

Once bingeing ceases and normal eating habits are restored, most people with bulimia will automatically stop purging. Some people, however, will need to make a special effort. For instance, don't eat anything you know you'll feel unable to keep down.

Recommended weight

In order to determine whether the amount of fat in your body is appropriate or excessive, doctors and dieticians use the Body Mass Index (BMI). BMI is calculated by the following equation: weight (in pounds) divided by height (in inches) squared, multiplied by 703. If you have access to the Internet, some websites work out the equation for you. (One such website is www.cdc.gov/nccdphp/dnpa/bmi/bmi-adult-formula.htm) The BMI for children and teenagers is different, the equation for which is also calculated on the above website.

Recommended weight ranges for adults are listed below.

Adult women. The figures given are in pounds.

Height	Small Frame	Medium Frame	Large Frame
4'09"	90–97	94–106	102–118
4'10"	92–100	97–109	105–121
4'11"	95–103	100–112	108–124
5'00"	98–106	103–115	111–127
5'01"	101–109	106–118	114–130
5'02"	104–112	109–122	117–134
5'03"	107–115	112–126	121–138
5'04"	110–119	116–131	125–142
5'05"	114–123	120–135	129–146
5'06"	118–127	124–139	133–150
5'07"	122–131	128–143	137–154
5'08"	126–136	132–147	141–159
5'09"	130–140	136–151	145–164
5'10"	133–144	140–155	149–169

Adult men. The figures given are in pounds.

Height	Small Frame	Medium Frame	Large Frame
5'01"	105–113	111–122	119–134
5'02"	108–116	114–126	122–137
5'03"	111–119	117–129	125–141
5'04"	114–122	120–132	128–145
5'05"	117–126	123–136	131–149
5'06"	121–130	127–140	135–154
5'07"	125–134	131–145	140–159
5'08"	129–138	135–149	144–163
5'09"	133–143	139–153	148–167
5'10"	137–147	143–158	152–172
5'11"	141–151	147–163	157–177
6'00"	145–155	151–173	166–187
6'01"	149–160	155–173	166–187
6'02"	153–164	160–178	171–192
6'03"	157–168	165–183	175–197

Changing to healthy eating

If you are recovering from an eating disorder and have successfully managed to incorporate five or six meals into your day, well done indeed! You may now wish to start eating more healthily. Looking at the sample menu below may help recovering compulsive eaters and recovering bulimics to replace the junk food with nutritious foods. Healthy eating will help you to keep off the weight you have already lost, and to lose more if you need to. Once you have reached your ideal weight for your sex, height and build, it is also excellent for stabilizing your weight. Good nutrition is great, too, for raising energy levels and improving overall health.

Eating more healthily is also of benefit to recovering alcoholics. Indeed, alcohol craving has been shown, in research, to be hugely reduced when nutritious foods are being consumed.

Drinks should include plenty of water, herbal teas and fresh fruit and vegetable juices. Ideally, fruit and vegetables should be organic, bread wholemeal, and any pre-packaged foods free from additives, including preservatives and colourings.

Note that the cup you should use for the measures given below is a small teacup or American cup measure rather than a mug.

Day 1
Breakfast: Grapefruit with a little muscovado sugar and 2 slices wholemeal toast
Snack: A wedge of melon
Lunch: A salad of your choice with scattered sunflower seeds
Snack: 1/3 cup dried apricots
Dinner: Irish stew with lean beef and plenty of vegetables
Snack: Two oatcakes (available from healthfood shops)

Day 2
Breakfast: Porridge with cracked linseed, raw honey and rice milk
Snack: Banana
Lunch: 2 soft-poached eggs on 2 slices of wholemeal toast
Snack: 1/3 cup pecan nuts mixed with sunflower seeds
Dinner: Grilled chicken breast with potatoes, carrots and green beans
Snack: Apple

Day 3
Breakfast: Grilled sardines on 2 slices of wholemeal toast
Snack: Carob bar (available from healthfood shops)
Lunch: Bean and vegetable soup with 2 wholemeal rolls, pear
Snack: 1/3 cup mixed dried fruit and nuts
Dinner: Homemade chicken curry with brown rice
Snack: 2 slices of soda bread, with butter and jam

Day 4
Breakfast: Bowl of raisin bran with soya milk, 2 slices of toast
Snack: 2 oatcakes
Lunch: Tuna salad, banana
Snack: 1/3 cup dried apricots
Dinner: Falafel (similar to a veggie burger and available from healthfood shops) with beans and homemade oven chips, orange
Snack: 2 farmhouse biscuits (available from healthfood shops)

Day 5

Breakfast:	Porridge with cracked linseed, rice milk and a little muscovado sugar
Snack:	1/3 cup pecan nuts
Lunch:	2 grilled kippers with 2 slices of wholemeal bread
Snack:	2 kiwi fruit
Dinner:	Mixed vegetable casserole
Snack:	2 slices wholemeal toast with honey

Day 6

Breakfast:	Fresh fruit salad, 1 oatcake
Snack:	2 Ryvita with cottage cheese
Lunch:	Scotch broth, apple
Snack:	1/3 cup mixed nuts
Dinner:	Tuna salad with 2 wholemeal rolls
Snack:	Orange

Day 7

Breakfast:	2 slices wholemeal toast with honey, banana
Snack:	2 rice cakes (available from healthfood shops)
Lunch:	Mixed salad, yogurt
Snack:	Pear
Dinner:	Baked wild salmon with potatoes, broccoli and carrots
Snack:	2 oat cakes

Changing from eating junk food to eating nutritionally can take a lot of effort and determination, so be warned! Eating is a pleasurable activity, we are used to choosing the foods that satisfy our taste buds – often made tastier by the addition of chemical flavourings and fat, sugar and salt – and you may be loath to make drastic changes. It is therefore recommended that you alter your eating habits gradually, taking just a few items from the sample menu per week in the early days. In this way, you allow yourself the time to adjust to the new textures, appearance and flavours of foods you are unaccustomed to. With perseverance, your tastes *will* change.

If you wish to start eating the new foods straightaway, I must add a word of warning. Nutritious, cleanly grown foods may trigger the body into instant detoxification – causing headaches, lethargy and even diarrhoea, lasting between one day and two weeks. You can avoid this shock to your system by making a gradual changeover.

When introducing this new way of eating, remember that it is important to consume a wide variety of foods. To eat the same things repeatedly means missing out on many vital building blocks of life, for certain foods build and regenerate only certain parts of the body.

If there are foods in the sample diet you just know you wouldn't eat on a regular basis, cut them out of your mind. A long-term healthy eating plan will only work if it is practical, sustainable and compatible with your lifestyle. If you feel it would be too difficult to change over to healthy eating on your own, you may prefer to ask your doctor for a referral to a dietician for additional help. Alternatively, there are many excellent nutritionists who can offer skilled guidance, for a fee.

Retraining your palate

In comparison with the average western diet that has, by the addition of chemical flavourings, saturated fat, sugar and salt, evolved largely to please the taste buds, a healthy diet is based on foods in their more natural form. It is advisable, therefore, that you *slowly* retrain your palate to accept different tastes. Cut back gradually on the amounts of sugar, salt and saturated fat you consume. It takes only 28 days of eating a food regularly for it to become a habit.

Keeping a diary

Keeping a food-intake diary is an excellent way to monitor the progress of your nutritional programme. I suggest that you buy a second notebook and devote a page to each day, listing all the foods you eat – including snacks and drinks.

Setting goals

It is a good idea to set small, achievable goals on the first page – that way you should get quicker results. For example, you may wish to make a goal of eating two types of vegetables each day. Without the diary, you may assume you've done badly, but upon reading your entries you may see that you've actually eaten two types of vegetables two or three times a week. That's a good starting point. Now you can focus on slowly increasing that amount.

Remember to not make too many changes in too short a time. This is not a 'fad' diet you are trying, this is hopefully a permanent lifestyle change, another step towards better health. Perhaps after setting a goal of eating more vegetables, you could set another of eating more fruit. Reducing foods with additives could maybe come next – with the aim of cutting them right down.

9

Improving Your Body Image and Self-Esteem

You are likely to have already acknowledged that you have a poor body image and low self-esteem and would like these things to be different, too. Starting with body image – the mental picture you have of your own body – it should be said that a person with an eating disorder may be almost as self-critical as someone with BDD. Some are even phobic about their bodies. Individuals who feel this way may avoid touching themselves or looking in the mirror. Self-esteem – one's basic emotional sense of self – is automatically raised when body image is improved.

Individuals with BDD are not only self-critical about their appearance, they have a distorted perception of their physical self, believing particular parts of their faces or bodies are ugly when really they are not – and it is their imagined physical flaws that are the chief cause of their low self-esteem. Improving body image is not easy for people with BDD, but it can certainly be done. Take your time in working through each of the following pointers. If you find them difficult to carry out, come back to them later. Remember that it takes time to develop a better body image.

If you suffer from alcoholism, you may also have a poor body image. Improving this aspect of your life can make a difference to the way you feel about yourself as a whole. It can raise your self-esteem.

- Think of a woman you admire, yet who is not excessively thin. What is it about her that makes you admire her? Is it her style, her wit, her confidence, her energy, her intelligence, her sense of purpose? Do you imagine that weight and shape are important to this person? If not, what do you think is important? Think of what it would take for you to cultivate her qualities, then make a determined effort to do so. If you are male, turn these questions around so they apply to you.
- Stand in front of a mirror and survey your reflection. You may immediately come up with a negative statement about your body, so compensate by making a positive one. There may not be much you like about yourself at this point, but force yourself to find something. Do this for every negative statement you make, every

time you look in a mirror. Now, most importantly, write down all your positive statements and, when you find yourself hating your body, read them through.

- Does your body image hold you back in any way? Do you avoid wearing skirts, looking in full-length mirrors, wearing swimwear or using a communal changing room? If the answer is 'yes', try looking at other women's bodies on the beach. Do they all have the perfect body? Would you swap with any one of them? The answer is probably 'no'. So why do you prefer your body to theirs? Write your answer in your notebook and keep referring to it. If you are male, change this paragraph around so that it applies to you.
- Start treating yourself to long hot baths, massaging aromatic oils into every inch of your skin afterwards. Linger a while on each part of your body and force yourself to counter every critical thought with a flattering one. For women, after each bath and oil application, paint your nails, style your hair and put on some make-up. Being kind to your body will have the gradual effect of you coming to like it.

Dealing with anxiety

Most people with an eating disorder, BDD or alcoholism suffer from anxiety. It can arise as a result of being unhappy about your body and weight, or general appearance, being locked into an unhealthy cycle of eating or drinking alcohol, worrying about what other people think of you or, in some cases, feeling isolated from family and friends.

You may be the type of person who finds certain situations very difficult to cope with – old friends calling to see you, for example. You may worry excessively about what to wear, what to talk about and what they will think of you. You may feel so bad you become sweaty and even panicky.

To determine whether you are currently an anxious person, think of how you were before your eating disorder, BDD or alcoholism, and ask yourself these questions:

- Am I more easily upset than I was?
- Do I feel that I overreact to certain situations?

- Am I more edgy than I was?
- Do I find it difficult to relax?
- Am I having more trouble sleeping than I was?
- In general, do I breathe more shallowly than before?

If you can answer 'yes' to any one of these questions, you are probably suffering from anxiety. Anxiety has the effect of stimulating the sympathetic nervous system – the mechanisms in the brain that respond automatically to certain occurrences – making you more tense, tired and anxious than previously. To help you become more relaxed, it is worth trying to follow a regular deep breathing and relaxation routine (see below).

When you find yourself in a difficult situation, it is also helpful to stay just where you are, however uncomfortable you may feel. In remaining within the situation, you will learn that it is tolerable and that your anxiety levels will gradually decrease. When you avoid a difficult situation, it is hard to believe you can bear the anxiety and that it can slowly ebb away.

Panic attacks

Acute hyperventilation – more commonly known as a panic attack – is fairly common in people with an eating disorder, BDD and alcoholism. A panic attack is an emotional response to anticipated stress. Often the perceived threat is obvious, but sometimes there is no apparent reason for the onset of panicky feelings. In the latter instance, the reason may be buried in earlier life events. Talking to a counsellor may unlock buried fears and help you to see them in a new, more manageable light.

As a rule, anxiety quickly intensifies before a panic attack. You will start breathing faster in troubled apprehension. Lightheadedness, palpitations, sweating, and the sensation that your chest is tightening will then be accompanied by feelings of inadequacy, fear and maybe of impending doom.

Daily deep breathing exercises – where breathing is slowed down and, on inhalation, the abdomen (not the ribcage) is allowed to rise – are very useful training. An immediate remedy is the good old paper bag. As soon as your breathing becomes fast and shallow, place the paper bag over your nose and mouth and try to breathe more slowly. Breathing into the bag will ensure that most of the exhaled carbon dioxide is returned to your lungs. It will also calm down your breathing.

Relaxation

Research indicates that people with stress-related problems like insomnia, anxiety and depression can have an oversensitive stress response and higher levels of stress hormones in their bloodstream than other people. This can affect your brain chemistry and be one factor in triggering and maintaining chronic stress, anxiety and depression. A useful strategy to learn is relaxation as it helps to halt the arousal of the sympathetic nervous system.

What actually is relaxation?

Many people think relaxation is sitting with their feet up watching the television or reading a book, but this is not strictly so. It is impossible to obtain the same beneficial biochemical and physiological changes while watching TV or reading a book as you do when practising relaxation. Indeed, research using EEG monitors to record the brainwave patterns of people watching television and others using a relaxation technique show that practising relaxation causes the brain to switch to alpha-type brainwaves that indicate true relaxation.

Deep breathing

In normal breathing, we take oxygen from the atmosphere down into our lungs. The diaphragm contracts, and air is pulled into the chest cavity. When we breathe out, we expel carbon dioxide and other waste gases back into the atmosphere. However, when we are stressed or upset, we tend to use the rib muscles to expand the chest. We breathe more quickly, sucking in shallowly. This is good in a crisis as it allows us to obtain the optimum amount of oxygen in the shortest possible time, providing our bodies with the extra power needed to handle the emergency. Some people do tend to get stuck in chest-breathing mode, though. Long-term shallow breathing is not only detrimental to our physical and emotional health, it can also lead to hyperventilation, panic attacks, chest pains, dizziness and gastro-intestinal problems.

To test your breathing, ask yourself:

- How fast are you breathing as you are reading this?
- Are you pausing between breaths?
- Are you breathing with your chest or with your diaphragm?

If you are breathing quickly and shallowly, it is recommended that you follow the deep breathing exercise given below.

A *deep breathing exercise*

The following exercise should, ideally, be performed daily:

1. Make yourself comfortable in a warm room where you know you will be alone for at least half an hour.
2. Close your eyes and try to relax.
3. Gradually slow down your breathing, inhaling and exhaling as evenly as possible.
4. Place one hand on your chest and the other on your abdomen, just below your ribcage.
5. As you inhale, allow your abdomen to swell upward (your chest should barely move).
6. As you exhale, let your abdomen flatten.

Give yourself a few minutes to get into a smooth, easy rhythm. As worries and distractions arise, don't hang on to them. Wait calmly for them to float out of your mind – then focus once more on your breathing.

When you feel ready to end the exercise, open your eyes. Allow yourself enough time to become alert before rolling onto one side and getting up. With practice, you will begin breathing with your diaphragm quite naturally – and in times of stress, you should be able to correct your breathing without too much effort.

A *relaxation exercise*

Relaxation is part of the balancing process together with other aspects of your lifestyle such as what you eat, your physical activity and how you handle stress. Learning to relax involves a little time and concentration but, unless you prefer to listen to a relaxation tape, these are the only costs involved.

Progressive muscular relaxation, which involves the active contracting and relaxing of muscles, is the most popular and easiest relaxation technique. When a muscle is tightened for a few seconds and then relaxed, the muscle returns to a more relaxed state. This process should be performed in the following parts of the body in turn.

1. Make yourself comfortable in a place where you will not be disturbed. (Listening to restful music may help you to relax.)
2. Begin to slow down your breathing, inhaling through your nose to a count of two.
3. Ensuring that the abdomen pushes outwards (as explained above) exhale to a count of four, five or six . . .
4. After a couple of minutes, concentrate on each part of the body in turn, starting with your left foot. Consciously tighten the muscles in the foot for four seconds, counting 'and one and two and three and four . . .' Now relax these same muscles, allowing the tension to flow right out . . . Let your foot feel heavier and heavier as every last remnant of tension seeps away . . . Follow this procedure with the right foot, then the legs, buttocks, stomach, back, shoulders, arms, hands, jaw and face.

Visualization

At this point, visualization can be introduced into the exercise. As you continue to breathe slowly and evenly, imagine yourself surrounded, perhaps, by lush, peaceful countryside, beside a gently trickling stream – or maybe on a deserted tropical beach, beneath swaying palm fronds, listening to the sounds of the ocean, thousands of miles from your worries and cares. Let the warm sun, the gentle breeze, the peacefulness of it all wash over you . . .

The tranquillity you feel at this stage can be enhanced by frequently repeating the exercise – once or twice a day is best. Given sufficient time, you should be able to switch into a calm state of mind whenever you feel stressed. Remember that relaxed muscles use far less energy than tense ones, and that improved breathing leads to better circulation and oxygenation which, in turn, helps the muscles and connective tissues. A relaxed mind can also greatly aid concentration and short-term memory. It can help eliminate 'brain fog', too.

Improving your relationships

It is important to consider how your personal relationships might be affected by your eating disorder, BDD or alcoholism. Some of you may have been able to preserve your relationships intact, but many others will have distanced yourselves both physically and emotionally. On the other hand, it may have been relationship problems that triggered your condition in the first place. All these scenarios are discussed in this section.

Making an effort

If you wish to improve your relationships with family members who are not living with you but with whom you were once close, this is a good time to renew contact. If visiting them is daunting, try a phone call – you'll be able to tell whether they want to chat. The chat may lead to a meeting, at which you are likely to find your relationship with that particular person restored.

Where past friends are concerned, it would be wise first of all to assess whether their presence in your life was worthwhile in the past i.e. was it a fifty–fifty relationship, or did you find yourself being the giver more than this particular person was. For example, were you the one who made all the running, who had to arrange things and was there to comfort the friend more than he or she was there to comfort you? If so, you might choose not to reinstate this friendship. However, if the friend was there for you as much as you were there for them, you will perhaps want to contact them once more. If even a phone call seems daunting, you could write a letter or send an email, which would give you the chance to explain your struggles with your problem, and that you are now on the road to recovery.

Assess all your past friendships in the same way, then review your current relationships with family and friends. Speaking openly of your struggles will undoubtedly have the effect of bringing them closer. It should make them want to assist you in your fight to recover. Having a rich and balanced network of relationships can be an enormous support, and is one of the most important ways of maintaining your well-being and psychological health.

Expressing yourself clearly

A problem such as an eating disorder, BDD or alcoholism may arise when parents find it difficult to express their feelings towards their child. Ongoing communication difficulties can then perpetuate the problem, whether the child is still a child, or now an adult. The individual may consequently feel they've had a lack of support.

In order to help your family to begin speaking openly, it can be a good idea to ask your doctor for a referral to a family therapy unit. Alternatively, if you feel brave enough, you can try to tackle the problem yourself. Should that fail, family therapy is always an option. Be careful how you word things, however. If, say, you feel that communication difficulties between your family and yourself is the root cause of a lot of your troubles, an accusation to that effect will only serve to alienate them further. You need to focus on the way you feel about their communication skills, then speak to them in a calm, non-confrontational, non-blaming way, as well as in a way that is constructive.

For example, you could say, 'We don't often talk to each other about how we feel, if we have problems and so on – but I would really like it if we could try to. I think that would help me to conquer my problem. What do you think?' You will probably receive an answer to the effect that of course they'll try to be more open, if it will help. Some parents might feel defensive and say, 'We do talk about how we feel!' Don't be too despondent if this happens. You are likely to find that, despite their protest, your parents will think about what you said and make an effort to be more open and supportive in the future. However, if there are no changes in the way your parents communicate with you and you think this has great bearing on your problem, family therapy is always an option. Speak to your doctor about this.

Encouraging someone close to change

If you feel family members or close friends contribute by their behaviour to your problem, speak to them about it. It's not always possible or healthy to remove such people from your lives, but it is possible to encourage them to change. But before you speak, do consider the following:

- *Ensure you have interpreted the other person's behaviour correctly.* For example, you may view your mother bringing you a basket of fruit and vegetables as a criticism of your diet – when in truth it is a goodwill gesture, just to show she cares. You have a perfect right to interpret the words or actions of others in whatever way you wish, but that interpretation is not necessarily reality. In fact, it is amazing (and common in eating and body image disorders) how wrong we often are in our perceptions of what others think and feel.
- *Ensure you are specific in recalling another person's behaviour.* For instance, 'You never understand how worried I am about my weight', is far more inflammatory than 'You didn't seem to

understand yesterday, when I told you I was worried about putting on three pounds.'

- *Try not to make an accusation.* For instance, 'I get so upset when you only think about yourselves!'; 'I don't believe you really care about me, and that makes me feel so hopeless!'; 'I'm losing my last shreds of confidence because you treat me as if I'm not trying to help myself!' Such comments will likely be seen as accusations; they may even provoke a quarrel. Speaking directly of your emotional requirements – without implying that the other person is contributing to your problems – will incline the person to take your comments more seriously. It should encourage more consideration in the future.

- *Ensure that what you are about to say is what you really mean.* For example, statements such as, 'Everyone thinks you're insensitive', 'We all think you've got an attitude problem' are, besides being inflammatory, very unfair. We have no way of knowing that 'everyone' is of the same opinion. The use of the depersonalized 'everyone', 'we' or 'us' – often said in the hope of deflecting the listener's anger – can cause more hurt and anger than if the criticism was direct and personal.

It is easy to see how others can misunderstand or take offence when we fail to communicate effectively. But changing the habits of a lifetime is difficult. It means analysing our thoughts before rearranging them into speech. You will be rewarded for your efforts, however, when people start to listen, when they start to support you in your efforts to conquer your problem. Most of all, if their behaviour had contributed to your problem, speaking carefully to them about it can make all the difference. If it doesn't, don't forget that your doctor can refer you to a local family unit for therapy.

10

Recovery Maintenance

The nature of eating disorders, BDD and alcoholism makes for a rocky road to recovery. Most of you will experience setbacks, whether you are helping yourselves or following trained guidance. It is more likely that you'll be able to get back on track if you've already developed a plan of action (see below).

It is normal for a person who is confronting an eating disorder or alcoholism to maintain a drive to either starve, binge-eat or drink alcohol. If you have kept surrendering to this drive, tell yourself that you have a choice over whether you give in or whether you continue with your recovery programme. When the preoccupation with food or drink is bad, or if you are recovering from BDD and begin to feel excessively anxious about your appearance, try to distract yourself by doing something you enjoy. This could be one of the following:

- Listen to a relaxation tape, or take yourself through the relaxation technique as described earlier, using visualization.
- Do some yoga. There are many instructional videos on the market, or courses available.
- Listen to music that either stirs you or relaxes you.
- Phone a friend or relative who makes you feel calm.
- Write a letter.
- Read a book.
- Play a musical instrument.
- Go for a drive.
- Draw or paint.
- Take a long bath.
- Give yourself a make-over.

Falling back into your old ways of thinking

If you find yourself constantly reverting to how you used to think, take a look again at your diary and reread your entries for 'Challenging negative thinking' and 'Problem-solving'. It's not easy to change entrenched thought patterns, but it can be done. Remember that with a little effort now, you will learn to see things in a more positive light, and that will help you to achieve a better body image. It will also help alcoholics to keep off the drink.

Self-help groups

There are now self-help groups for people with eating disorders and alcohol problems. Overeaters Anonymous is firmly established, and groups for people with anorexia and bulimia are slowly increasing in number. Alcoholics Anonymous remains an excellent self-help group for recovering alcoholics, and I would advise any alcoholic to join them.

One advantage of a self-help group is that the person doesn't feel like a patient with a 'disease', unlike when attending a hospital. Everyone at the group is in the same situation. Furthermore, self-help groups often have members who are available at all times via a telephone helpline, acting as crisis management for their fellow members. Members act as a general support network for each other – and, for those who can offer help, their self-esteem is raised. Self-help groups also offer the opportunity to make new friends you can see socially, outside the group.

It is important that you don't depend entirely on a self-help group for guidance and support. Self-help groups can, however, be a beneficial adjunct to the advice in this book. You can also attend a self-help group while receiving treatment from a professional.

Unfortunately, there appear to be no self-help groups as yet specifically for people with BDD. However, you may wish to join a group for individuals with an anxiety disorder or one that supports people with obsessive-compulsive disorder. (See Useful Addresses.)

Seeking outside help

You may have read through the different advice for self-help treatment and be convinced that your problem is too severe for you to tackle alone. Alternatively, you may have tried hard repeatedly to follow the instructions and failed every time. The only answer, in both cases, is for you to find outside help.

When you visit your doctor, you will be asked a series of questions in order to determine the severity of your condition. A decision will then be made between yourself and the doctor as to whether you are prescribed anti-depressants, referred for Cognitive

Behavioural Therapy (see below) as out-patient treatment, or referred for in-patient treatment at a hospital or special unit.

Anti-depressants

Research has shown that anti-depressants can be of enormous benefit to people with the problems discussed in this book. Patients become less focused on their particular addiction or phobia and their general mood greatly improves. People who binge-eat, drink alcohol or obsess about their appearance do so with far less intensity and frequency – however, anti-depressants cannot stop them doing so altogether.

The drugs currently being prescribed for people with an eating disorder, BDD and alcoholism are either tricyclic anti-depressants such as imipramine, desipramine and amitriptyline; monoamine oxidase inhibitors such as phenelzine; or Selective Serotonin Re-uptake Inhibitors (SSRIs) such as fluoxetine and fluvoxamine. Nowadays, it is usually SSRIs that are prescribed first of all for the disorders in this book. If one anti-depressant fails to be of benefit, your doctor will be able to prescribe another. It is important, therefore, that you keep your doctor informed of your response.

Cognitive Behavioural Therapy

A fairly new psychological treatment, Cognitive Behavioural Ther-apy (CBT) is an important approach to the treatment of all types of eating disorder, as well as for BDD and alcoholism. If you are open to change, the treatment can be very successful. Skilled therapists are warm, positive, empathetic and honest, and a sense of teamwork is normally established quite quickly. You are involved in all clinical decision-making and encouraged to give regular feedback about your treatment and progress. Central to the CBT approach is restructuring the thought processes that maintain your disorder, as a result of which you will come to challenge the thoughts that led to your problem.

You will also be taught the following:

- How to challenge negative thinking.
- How to chart your progress in overcoming a core negative belief.
- How to keep a diary of your observations which are consistent with your new beliefs.
- How to raise your self-esteem.

If you have an eating disorder, you will also be taught the following:

- How to plan your meals.
- How to monitor your eating.

Good luck! Remember, with support and determination, eating disorders and poor body image *can* be overcome!

References

Biery, J. R., Williford, J. H., McMullen, E. A., 'Alcohol craving in rehabilitation: assessment of nutrition therapy', *Journal of the American Dieticians Association* 1991, 91:463–6.

Guenther R. M., 'Role of nutritional therapy in alcoholism treatment', *International Journal of Biosocial Research* 1983, 4:5–18.

Kolb, L. C., 'Disturbances of the Body Image', *The American Handbook of Psychiatry*, 1959, 1:749–69.

Wertheim, E. et al. 'Psychosocial predictors of weight loss behaviours and binge eating in adolescents', *International Journal of Eating Disorders*, cited in Queensland Health Promotion Council 'Give me back my body' Sunshine Coast Body Image and Eating Behaviours Project, 1997.

Useful Addresses

Addaction
Central Office
67–69 Cowcross Street
London EC1M 6PU
Tel.: 020 7251 5860
Fax: 020 7251 5890
Website: www.addaction.org.uk
Email: info@addaction.org.uk
Works in the field of drug and alcohol treatment.

Alcohol Concern
Waterbridge House
32–36 Loman Street
London SE1 0EE
Tel.: 020 7928 7377
Fax: 020 7928 4644
Website: www.alcoholconcern.org.uk
Email: contact@alcoholconcern.org.uk

Alcoholics Anonymous
P.O. Box 1
Stonebow House
Stonebow
York
YO1 7NJ
National helpline: 0845 769 7555
Website: www.alcoholics-anonymous.org.uk

Drinkline
Helpline: 0800 917 8282 (24 hours a day, 7 days a week)
The national alcohol helpline.

First Steps to Freedom
1 Taylor Close
Kenilworth
Warwickshire CV8 2LW

Tel.: 01926 864473 (general enquiries)
Helpline: 0845 120 2916 (10 am–10 pm)
Website: www.first-steps.org
Email: first.steps@btconnect.com
Practical help for people who suffer from anorexia, bulimia, phobias, obsessive-compulsive disorder, general anxiety and panic attacks.

International Association of Anxiety Management
Website: www.anxman.org
Email: enquiries@panic-anxicty.com
A web resource for sufferers of all anxiety disorders, phobias and panic.

Mental Health Foundation
London Office
20 Upper Ground
London
SE1 9QB
Tel.: 020 7803 1100
Fax: 020 7803 1111
Website: www.mentalhealth.org.uk
Email: mhf@mhf.org.uk

National Centre for Eating Disorders
54 New Road
Esher
Surrey
KT10 9NU
Tel.: 0845 838 2040
Website: www.eating-disorders.org.uk

Norfolk Eating Disorders Association
The Colegate Centre
34 Colegate
Norwich
Norfolk
NR3 1BG
Tel.: 01603 767 062
Website: www.norfolkeda.org.uk
Email: support@norfolkeda.org.uk

Overeaters Anonymous
(For help and information)
PO Box 19
Stretford
Manchester
M32 9EB
Helpline: 07000 784985

(Registered Office)
9 Thorpe Close
Portobello Road
London W10 5NL
Website: www.oagb.org.uk

OCD Action
22–24 Highbury Grove
Suite 107
London N5 2EA
Help and Information Line 0870 766 7600
Tel.: 020 7226 4545 (office)
Fax: 020 7288 0828
Website: www.ocdaction.org.uk
Email: info@ocdaction.org.uk
Information and support for Obsessive-Compulsive Disorder (OCD) and the related disorders of Body Dysmorphic Disorder (BDD) and Compulsive Skin Picking (CSP).

Samaritans
Helpline: 08457 90 90 90 (UK)
Helpline: 1850 60 90 90 (Republic of Ireland)
Administrative Office Tel.: 020 8394 8300
Website: www.samaritans.org.uk
Email: jo@samaritans.org

Chris
PO Box 90 90
Stirling
FK8 2SA
(Specifically for writing to Samaritans)

Overseas

Alcoholics Anonymous
General Service Office
Website: www.alcoholics-anonymous.org
(Serving Alcoholics Anonymous in the USA and Canada)

BDD Central
Website: www.bddcentral.com

National Eating Disorders Association (NEDA)
603 Stewart Street
Suite 803
Seattle
WA 98101
USA
Tel.: (206) 382-3587
Website: www.nationaleatingdisorders.org
Email: info@nationaleatingdisorders.org

Further Reading

Cash, Thomas F., *The Body Image Workbook: An 8-step Program for Learning to Like your Looks.* New Harbinger Publications, London, 1997.

Edwards, Griffith, *Alcohol: The World's Favorite Drug.* St Martin's Press, USA, 2003.

Fairburn, Christopher G., *Overcoming Binge Eating.* Guilford Press, London, 1995.

Freeman, Christopher, *Overcoming Anorexia Nervosa.* Constable and Robinson, London, 2002.

McCabe, Randi et al., *The Overcoming Bulimia Workbook: Your comprehensive, step-by-step guide to recovery.* New Harbinger Publications, USA, 2004.

Phillips, Katherine A., The *Broken Mirror: Understanding and Treating Body Dysmorphic Disorder.* Oxford University Press Inc., USA, 2005.

Treasure, Janet, Schmidt, Ulrike, van Furth, Eric, *The Essential Handbook of Eating Disorders.* John Wiley and Sons, London, 2005.

Index

THE LEARNING CENTRE
HAMMERSMITH AND WEST
LONDON COLLEGE
GLIDDON ROAD
LONDON W14 9BL